SCRIPTURAL ROO

COMMERCE

BOOK 4

WORKING TOGETHER

JIM PETERSEN

WITH

DONALD MCGILCHRIST
TOM PETERSEN
JERRY WHITE
GLENN MCMAHAN, EDITOR

THIRD EDITION

Global Commerce Network
P.O. Box 51455
Colorado Springs, CO 80949-1455
www.globalcommercenetwork.com
info@globalcommercenetwork.com

International Standard Book Number (ISBN): 978-0-9860918-5-8

First Edition February 2003. Third Edition published in 2015.

The quotations from sources other than the Scriptures have been chosen to amplify or stimulate further thought. They are not necessarily consistent with a biblical worldview.

Proofreading by Kathy Petersen

Printed in the United States of America

CONTENTS

FOREWORD

To link the words "Scriptural" and "Commerce" in the title of a book series may seem odd to today's popular mindset. Even in Christian circles, many people assume that the Scriptures have little to say about business, innovation, or daily work. This assumption, unfortunately, is based on a long history of misguided thinking that divided our lives into "secular" and "sacred" compartments. This fragmentation has its consequences. Separating theology from the workplace has frustrated many working men and women, leaving them to feel that their professional lives have no significance in relation to God's purposes in the world.

Having experienced this frustration first-hand, a group of theologians and businessmen set out in the mid-1990s to research what the Scriptures teach about work and commerce. Over the course of six years, they discovered what author Paul Minear stated so well: "The Bible is a book by workers, about workers, for workers." Inspired by what they learned, the original team published the *Scriptural Roots of Commerce*. What you are reading now is the third version of the "SRC," as it's commonly known.

What is commerce? In our view, commerce includes the broad scope of all economic activity at every level. This definition involves all professions—medicine, teaching, science, construction, military, mining, law. Commerce covers a vast array of interactions. It is highly relational. It plays a significant role in forming the culture in which we live. In fact, very little happens in life without commerce.

God gives us the freedom and responsibility to shape our world (for better or worse). So, as we engage in commerce, our decisions and actions matter not just for our own lives, but also for our communities and even the next generation. This sobering responsibility should compel us to rethink the status quo and to pay close attention to what God desires for work and commerce. After all, he reveals his designs for life not to constrain us but to help us thrive. The Scriptures reveal a God who cares about commerce because he cares about people.

The *Scriptural Roots of Commerce* provides a practical and accessible framework to help you explore work and commerce through the lens of the Scriptures. The books will not give you canned answers that force you toward predetermined outcomes, but will help you explore and think about what the Scriptures reveal about your professional life.

Obviously, these books require your time and commitment. We believe this is one of the best attributes of the series! In our hurried and impatient world, we are tempted to skim across an ocean of superficial information, filling our heads with unrelated facts and applying very little of what we learn. Our attention spans wane under an onslaught of unrelated sound-bites, tweets, and ads. The cacophony presents us with no purposeful, over-arching story. Not surprisingly, we long for meaning. By contrast, the SRC will help you build your worldview and grow as a person. It encourages us to slow down, think deeply, and live innovatively alongside a committed group of close friends.

Our hope is expressed in our mission statement: "to help men and women align their lives with biblical truth, so that they can survive and flourish in the workplace and spread purpose and hope within their contexts."

Glenn McMahan
Chairman
Global Commerce Network

GETTING THE MOST OUT OF THIS STUDY

The Scriptural Roots of Commerce offers a sequence for developing your thinking about the most critical matters of human life. Book 1 takes us toward a deeper understanding of God, the foundation for everything else. Book 2 helps us better comprehend human nature and what that means for the way we live and work. Book 3 presents the kingdom of God within which our lives find meaning and hope. The fourth book unveils the crucial role of relationships in commerce, and God's design for our relationships. Book 5 presents a theology of work that helps us understand why work is meaningful. The last book in the series offers a much needed biblical understanding of wealth and finances.

We recommend that you work through the books according to the sequence described above. However, depending on your interests and needs, the books can be used out of order.

Importantly, the SRC is designed to be studied with peers. We learn and grow best in iron-sharpens-iron friendships. Participants often provide excellent (and free) life coaching and business consulting for one another.

Although the SRC stimulates serious thinking, it is not only an intellectual exercise. What we learn should be lived, and what we live helps us learn. We encourage you to think creatively about how to apply what you learn from the Scriptures in your workplace and community.

Forming an SRC group is simple. It only takes someone to make the invitations, set a time and place, and create an environment where people feel free to bring questions and insights. The SRC provides the content and the basic structure. Because the SRC is about discovery, facilitators don't need to have all the answers. If you would like to start a group, Global Commerce Network has published a Facilitator's Guide to help.

Many people ask how long it takes to go through the series. What's the hurry? Some groups study a section at home before meeting together. Others prefer to read and discuss small sections for the first time during each meeting. The important thing is to take your time, think deeply, live what you learn, and enjoy the friendships.

If you need help, write us at: info@globalcommercenetwork.com.

OVERVIEW OF THE SRC

The subject matter in these six books is broad enough to shape not only the way we work, but also our approach to every sphere of life. The first three books focus on aligning our worldview with the truth of the Gospel. The last three books help us apply this understanding in our relationships, work, and economy.

Book 1: Why God Matters

What we believe about God affects everything, including our work. This book unveils God's nature, giving us an opportunity to explore his creativity, entrepreneurial spirit, justice, love, and forgiveness. A growing relationship with God will have a dramatic impact on our professional and personal lives.

Book 2: Why People Matter

All work and commerce is an expression of human nature. People are capable of amazing goodness, but we struggle with deep undercurrents of selfishness, greed, envy, and even hatred. If we don't have a realistic understanding of human nature, it will be difficult to make sense of our lives or the workplace. A true view of who we are will improve our ability to renew the workplace so that people and businesses thrive.

Book 3: Life in the Kingdom

The kingdom of God is the big picture. It is the stage upon which God and people interact. It's the arena in which God fulfills his purposes. We need to understand God's kingdom and his purposes to have a true perspective about the world around us and how we are to live. God calls us to live and work as citizens of his kingdom even though it often exists in tension with our culture.

Book 4: Working Together

All commerce is relational. We relate to clients, suppliers, colleagues, bosses, and employees. Surprisingly, most companies never give the relational element of commerce much thought. But if we can relate well in the workplace (and at home) by growing in character traits such as humility, integrity, and forgiveness, our lives and work will flourish.

Book 5: The Meaning of Work

We spend most of our lives working. Do our jobs mean anything to God? The Meaning of Work offers a positive answer to that question. Early in the story, we discover a God who works and who has designed us to work. We explore the truth that all work done in faith is sacred and purposeful. The study then helps us discover how our professional lives can be integrated with God's restoration of a broken world. It closes with an investigation of physical and spiritual rest in the context of our stressful times.

Book 6: The Economy of God

In this study, we explore a biblical perspective of material and spiritual wealth. God's material world provides a capital base that we can use for the glory of God by working it and caring for it. In God's economy, even those who are materially poor can be spiritually rich, and those who are materially wealthy might find they are spiritually poor.

THE IMPORTANCE OF YOUR WORLDVIEW

This study, without imposing a dogma, helps you understand and re-think your worldview in light of the Scriptures. So, it might be helpful to understand how your deepest beliefs affect your life.

Worldview: A worldview is a composite of beliefs, usually adopted from one's culture, media, traditions, family, education, and religion. Every person has a worldview, even if it has been formed in an *ad hoc* manner. It shapes the way we see and interpret reality, the way we answer the big questions of life: How do I understand the world and its origins? Who am I? What makes life meaningful? What is my belief about God? What happens after death?

Values: Our worldview influences our values. A value is something so important to us that it motivates our actions and decisions. If, for example, I believe there is no life after death, that belief will influence what I find to be most important. Living for the moment, a *carpe diem* approach to life, would probably be my ambition.

Behavior: In this way, our worldview and values shape our behavior and choices. If self-fulfillment is our primary driving value, our behavior will follow. We will spend a lot of time and energy pursuing things that we hope will satisfy that desire. So, our choices and actions each day reflect something about what we really believe.

These three factors serve as a basic framework for understanding our-selves and our society. They also instruct us in how to grow and change. Trying to change just our behavior without addressing our beliefs will usu-ally fail because nothing has changed in our minds and hearts!

Worldview is not just a matter of the intellect. The Bible says: "Above all else, guard your heart, for it is the wellspring of life" (Proverbs 4:23). So, what you believe about God is influenced by your will and heart. The Scrip-tures make it clear that if a person's heart is bent on maintaining indepen-dence from God, all the best arguments in favor of God won't change any-thing. The intellect is crucial, but there must also be humility in the heart.

The SRC begins by expanding our understanding of God in order to align our lives with him, the sole source of life. As we do this, every area of our lives will be enriched. How do you answer the big questions?

WHAT IS THE BIBLE?

The Bible is without a doubt the most influential book in all of history. Basing their lives on the Bible, men and women have established constitutional governments, opposed totalitarian regimes, ended slavery, developed science, founded universities, worked to cure sickness, served the poor, fought against racism, and humanized commerce. Most importantly, the Bible has been the cornerstone for establishing the infinite and unconditional worth of every human being.

The Bible is a collection of books, a library, written over a period of 1,600 years from approximately B.C. 1500 to A.D. 100. Its contents are inextricably rooted in history. The Bible accurately presents specific and testable details about kings, construction, battles, cities, and currencies.

The books of the Bible also portray the full spectrum of human nature. In prose and poetry, the authors express their deepest longings and questions. Others publicly confess their worst behavior and attitudes. King David's adultery, Peter's denial of Christ, Paul's violence against the early church—it's all there for us to read. Clearly, the Bible was not written by public relations specialists trying to put a positive spin on religious ideas. Instead, the Bible is authentic and honest, addressing the complexities and questions faced by every person.

About forty different authors contributed to the Bible. The writers include farmers, soldiers, prophets, kings, musicians, statesmen, fishermen, doctors, and apostles. Given the diversity of the authors and the time-span of the writings, one would expect to find an unintelligible hodgepodge of conflicting ideas. To the contrary, there is amazing congruence, with each part contributing to a single, central story. This story is about a just and holy God taking every initiative to show us who he is, what he's like, and how we can live whole and meaningful lives. His motive? He loves us!

The Old Testament provides the history of God's involvement with the nations, primarily with the Israelites. God gradually reveals his holiness, justice, and love. He communicates through the beauty and order of the physical universe, through his messengers (who often wound up murdered), and through his tangible action in history. Many chapters foretell the coming of Jesus, some in great detail. By the time Jesus arrived, most Jewish people knew exactly how to recognize him when they saw him.

The New Testament begins with four accounts of Jesus' life, each from a slightly different perspective. These books are called the Gospels. Then, in the book of Acts, there is a detailed account of the birth of the young churches that sprang up across the Roman Empire in the first century. The remainder of the New Testament consists of personal letters that helped the early faith communities to thrive as followers of Christ.

One of those letters, written by Peter, explains why the Scriptures are so extraordinary: "Above all, you must understand that no prophecy of Scripture came about by the prophet's own interpretation. For prophecy never had its origin in the will of man, but men spoke from God as they were carried along by the Holy Spirit."

Because the Bible is thus inspired, it gives us God's wisdom for living a meaningful and joyful life. It addresses issues such as relationships, emotional health, child rearing, work, business, finances, leadership, and government. As you become familiar with the Bible and benefit from its matchless wisdom, you will understand the importance of Peter's words.

May you be inspired to build, innovate, and serve as you interact with the Bible.

WORKING TOGETHER
INTRODUCTION

The first three books in this series establish the foundations for a biblical worldview. They give us a framework for understanding life and for making sense of what it's about. They help us understand who God is, who we are as human beings, and the overarching narrative of God's purposes. We are participants in the great eternal drama.

These three books have established the foundations for everything else in life. Now we're ready to investigate what this means for our daily lives. For most of us, everyday life revolves around three things: people, work, and material resources. How we do in these areas—the way we relate to the people in our lives, how we approach our work and how we manage our resources—must be aligned with the kingdom and purposes of God. As that alignment takes place, we will be increasingly in tune with what God requires of us.

The People in Our Lives

While praying to His Father, Jesus said, "Now this is eternal life: that they may know you, the only true God, and Jesus Christ, whom you have sent" (John 17:3). Our lives must be founded on a relationship with God through Jesus Christ. The impact of this primary relationship expands out to and enriches all subsequent relationships.

Life is about relationships. We work and manage our material assets to provide for ourselves, our families, and others. We expend time and energy nurturing our social relationships, such as our friendships with neighbors and business associates. We even try to keep track of our high school classmates. People are important to us. When we near the end and look back at it all, the people we shared our lives with will be the most significant aspect. Our regrets will be over relationships that didn't go well. Our other achievements, whatever they might have been, will be secondary.

It is difficult for us to keep this priority in focus. The consuming demands of business, the concentration required to keep it on track, and the daily pressures of life and its myriad of responsibilities all work together to coerce many people into living for some other purpose. There are also people who willingly sacrifice relationships for something else, like professional success. They pay for this success with failure in their relationships. So, we have to ask: Are they really successful?

Part of our problem with keeping relationships in focus is that we are dealing with a cultural blind spot. We are not good at relationships, and we don't know it!

This lack of attention to and understanding of relationships impacts work and commerce in profound ways. All commerce is relational, on the macro and micro levels. We relate with clients, colleagues, bosses. Healthy businesses thrive in part because they build trust with other businesses through integrity. Many a business has failed because of relational breakdown born from pride. And people in the workplace often languish simply because the work environment is so impersonal, or downright cruel. Despite these facts, very little attention is given to improving the relational foundations upon which all commerce occurs.

Individualism: A Cultural Blind Spot

How can we see the people in our lives for who they really are when we have been born and bred on hyper-individualism? Individualism is the belief that a person can live without needing others. This extreme self-centeredness is one of the ideas that we inherited from the Renaissance.

In medieval society, personal identity was defined at birth by the context to which you belonged—which church, which family, or which landowner. Individuality was valued less than today. The Renaissance brought increased self-awareness, faith in the individual's capacity to create and achieve. Leonardo de Vinci, Michelangelo, Christopher Columbus, Copernicus, and Martin Luther, all of whom lived within the span of a single generation (1490 to 1520), brought people to new levels of personal freedom. Each, in his own way, affirmed and elevated the individual. Together, they set in motion a trend that continues to this day.

Individuality is an important idea. The Scriptures teach us to value the individual. They teach us that people have both the right and the responsibility to think and to choose for themselves. It is when we carry this truth to the extreme, when we make it an "ism," that we run into trouble.

The doctrine of individualism promotes the notion that the pursuit of self-fulfillment is the highest good—that this is something we owe ourselves. We make heroes of those among us who seem to succeed at this. We admire people like J.P. Morgan or Steve Jobs whose entrepreneurial achievements seem to have been done single-handedly. But the fact is, great entrepreneurs never survive alone. They could not have succeeded without a supportive community.

So, radical individualism is a facade. Is it success when we sacrifice one part of our lives for achievement in another? Because we believe this myth and pursue it, we justify our selfish lifestyles and excuse the neglect of the people in our lives for the sake of the chase! Men, especially, in our society tend to have very few friends. Instead, they have competitors and customers. As we live out the myth, we drive to work alone. At day's end we retreat into our private media world where we relax alone. The kids have their own electronic gadgets so they won't bother us. We have constructed a society that accommodates and perpetuates this myth that self-promotion is the road to fulfillment.

Why are we surprised that we find it so hard to make marriages and childrearing work? Why is it that, although we live surrounded by people, we still feel somehow disconnected and isolated? Why are so many relationships conflict-ridden?

1. Can you identify with this description of our society? What would you add? What would you delete?

2. Is there a relationship in your life that you feel you need to improve, or that needs reconciliation? Write down the name of the person and what you'd like to see happen. Keep the relationship in mind as you work through this book.

Section 1
Be Imitators of God

The very notion of a relationship comes from God. He created us to mirror his attributes. He is personal and relational, and we are made in his image. God loves, mourns, and enjoys. So do we. But there has been a breakdown between God and us. God is holy, we are not. We are, in fact, so far from being holy that it's hard for us to understand why he makes such a big deal over our sins. But we would not drink water if we knew it had just one drop of sewage. Likewise, God couldn't remain holy if he accepted us in our broken condition.

This breakdown in our relationship with God carries over into every other relationship we have. In spite of our best intentions, we find ourselves doing and saying things that further estrange the very people we most desperately love. Our frustrations, anger, and other sins seem to have a life of their own. We feel helpless and unable to respond as we know we should.

Reconciliation is the central message of the Scriptures. "God was reconciling the world to himself in Christ. . . " (2 Corinthians 5:19). In Christ, God has repaired the irreparable. The way back to a relationship with him has been restored. It follows that this reconciliation, this restoration, which is ours from God, should also permeate our relationships with the people in our lives.

God has shown how we can restore and enrich our relationships with others. The things he did and the attitudes he displayed as he moved to reconcile us to himself serve as guideposts for our response to him—and to every other person to whom we relate. He is our model for relationships!

In this section we will explore four characteristics that we observe in God as he reconciles us to himself. They are:

- Holiness and justice
- Love
- Humility
- Forgiveness

Why these four, we ask? It is because each of these has been singled out in the Scriptures for us to imitate. We are told:

- Holiness and justice: ". . . be like God in true righteousness and holiness" (Ephesians 4:24).
- Love: ". . . love one another. As I have loved you. . . "(John 13:34).
- Humility: "Your attitude should be the same as that of Christ Jesus. . . . He humbled himself. . ." (Philippians 2:5, 8).
- Forgiveness ". . . forgiving each other, just as in Christ God forgave you" (Ephesians 4:32).

"Be imitators of God . . ." (Ephesians 5:1). That's our thesis. By examining the character traits God displayed as he reconciled us to himself, we learn how to relate back to him—and how to relate to every other person in our lives. We begin to understand the beauty, the richness, of true relationships. In fact, these four characteristics are the critical path to reconciliation with both God and the people in our lives.

In the Scriptures, God has given us all we need to blend these qualities into our own lives. He also gives us the Holy Spirit who empowers us to live accordingly. In this section our purpose is to gain a better understanding of what these four characteristics really mean—so that we can consciously, intentionally, make them a part of our lives.

A. Holiness and Justice

Just about the first thing we learn about God is that he is holy. The forty years that the nation of Israel spent in the desert going from Egypt to Canaan could be described as a course in how to survive living together with a holy God. Leviticus, the book many of us prefer to skim over in our Bible reading, was essential reading for the Israelites. It is an exposition on the theme: "Be holy because I, the Lord your God, am holy" (Leviticus 19:2). It taught the Israelites to value human life, to assume responsibility for their own behavior, to be humane, just, sexually moral, and even orderly!

1. It is difficult for us to grasp how significant it is that God is holy. The following scriptures help us. Watch for the qualities that are inherent in God's holiness.

PSALM 9:7–8

The Lord reigns forever; he has established his throne for judgment. He will judge the world in righteousness; he will govern the peoples with justice.

PSALM 72:1–4

Endow the king with your justice, O God, the royal son with your righteousness. He will judge your people in righteousness, your afflicted ones with justice. The mountains will bring prosperity to the people, the hills the fruit of righteousness. He will defend the afflicted among the people and save the children of the needy; he will crush the oppressor.

PSALM 96:13

. . . they will sing before the Lord, for he comes, he comes to judge the earth. He will judge the world in righteousness and the peoples in his truth.

PSALM 97:2

Clouds and thick darkness surround him; righteousness and justice are the foundation of his throne.

> Justice refers to behavior whereas righteousness has to do with character. Justice is righteousness in action.

PSALM 99:1-5

The Lord reigns, let the nations tremble; he sits enthroned between the cherubim, let the earth shake. Great is the Lord in Zion; he is exalted over all the nations. Let them praise your great and awesome name—he is holy. The King is mighty, he loves justice—you have established equity; in Jacob you have done what is just and right. Exalt the Lord our God and worship at his footstool; he is holy.

ISAIAH 5:16

But the Lord Almighty will be exalted by his justice, and the holy God will show himself holy by his righteousness.

ISAIAH 11:3-5

. . . and he will delight in the fear of the Lord. He will not judge by what he sees with his eyes, or decide by what he hears with his ears; but with righteousness he will judge the needy, with justice he will give decisions for the poor of the earth. He will strike the earth with the rod of his mouth; with the breath of his lips he will slay the wicked. Righteousness will be his belt and faithfulness the sash around his waist.

JEREMIAH 23:5-6

"The days are coming," declares the Lord, "when I will raise up to David a righteous Branch, a King who will reign wisely and do what is just and right in the land. In his days Judah will be saved and Israel will live in safety. This is the name by which he will be called: The Lord Our Righteousness."

> Creation tells us that we owe our existence to a holy God whose character is the standard of all righteousness, the measure of all morality. 'Be holy because I, the Lord your God, am holy' (Lev. 19:2). The clear failing of the secular worldview is that it tells us we owe our existence to natural forces acting at random; therefore, there can be no ultimate source of moral norms. *Charles Colson*

JOHN 18:36–39

Jesus said, "My kingdom is not of this world. If it were, my servants would fight to prevent my arrest by the Jews. But now my kingdom is from another place."

"You are a king, then!" said Pilate.

Jesus answered, "You are right in saying I am a king. In fact, for this reason I was born, and for this I came into the world, to testify to the truth. Everyone on the side of truth listens to me."

"What is truth?" Pilate asked. With this he went out again to the Jews and said, "I find no basis for a charge against him. But it is your custom for me to release to you one prisoner at the time of the Passover. Do you want me to release 'the king of the Jews'?"

1.1 How is God's holiness expressed?

1.2 What difference does it make that God relates to us with justice and righteousness?

1.3 How should holiness shape our values and conduct in the workplace?

ᥬ

We almost never use the word "holy" to describe another person. We reserve its use for when we're talking about God—and then we're not sure what we really mean. But in the following scriptures three words are repeatedly used as being descriptive of holiness, and we have a good idea of what they mean. They are: righteousness, justice, and truth. When God calls us to "be holy," he is calling us to love righteousness, to act justly, and to live out truth. The following scriptures will help us understand how that should look.

2. How should knowing that God is holy affect our relationships?

PSALM 15:1–5

Lord, who may dwell in your sanctuary? Who may live on your holy hill? He whose walk is blameless and who does what is righteous, who speaks the truth from his heart and has no slander on his tongue, who does his neighbor no wrong and casts no slur on his fellowman, who despises a vile man but honors those who fear the Lord, who keeps his oath even when it hurts, who lends his money without usury and does not accept a bribe against the innocent. He who does these things will never be shaken.

PROVERBS 12:17–20
A truthful witness gives honest testimony, but a false witness tells lies. Reckless words pierce like a sword, but the tongue of the wise brings healing. Truthful lips endure forever, but a lying tongue lasts only a moment. There is deceit in the hearts of those who plot evil, but joy for those who promote peace.

PROVERBS 25:11–15
A word aptly spoken is like apples of gold in settings of silver. Like an earring of gold or an ornament of fine gold is a wise man's rebuke to a listening ear. Like the coolness of snow at harvest time is a trustworthy messenger to those who send him; he refreshes the spirit of his masters. Like clouds and wind without rain is a man who boasts of gifts he does not give. Through patience a ruler can be persuaded, and a gentle tongue can break a bone.

Integrity comes from the verb to integrate, which means to become united so as to form a complete or perfect whole. *Charles Colson*

JEREMIAH 22:13–17
Woe to him who builds his palace by unrighteousness, his upper rooms by injustice, making his countrymen work for nothing, not paying them for their labor. He says, 'I will build myself a great palace with spacious upper rooms.' So he makes large windows in it, panels it with cedar and decorates it in red. Does it make you a king to have more and more cedar? Did not your father have food and drink? He did what was right and just, so all went well with him. He defended the cause of the poor and needy, and so all went well. Is that not what it means to know me? . . . But your eyes and your heart are set only on dishonest gain, on shedding innocent blood and on oppression and extortion.

. . . the humble person will stick both to truth and to love. He will stick to the Word of God and let it lead to his brother. Because he seeks nothing for himself and has no fears for himself, he can help his brother through the Word. *Dietrich Bonhoeffer*

EPHESIANS 4:20–25
. . . Surely you heard of him and were taught in him in accordance with the truth that is in Jesus. You were taught, with regard to your former way of life, to put off your old self, which is being corrupted by its deceitful desires; to be made new in the attitude of your minds; and to put on the new self, created to be like God in true righteousness and holiness. Therefore each of you must put off falsehood and speak truthfully to his neighbor, for we are all members of one body.

EPHESIANS 6:13–18

Therefore put on the full armor of God, so that when the day of evil comes, you may be able to stand your ground, and after you have done everything, to stand. Stand firm then, with the belt of truth buckled around your waist, with the breast-plate of righteousness in place, and with your feet fitted with the readiness that comes from the gospel of peace. In addition to all this, take up the shield of faith, with which you can extinguish all the flaming arrows of the evil one. Take the hel-met of salvation and the sword of the Spirit, which is the word of God. And pray in the Spirit on all occasions with all kinds of prayers and requests. With this in mind, be alert and always keep on praying for all the saints.

HEBREWS 12:14

Make every effort to live in peace with all men and to be holy; without holiness no one will see the Lord.

2.1 We have been reflecting on large concepts: justice, righteousness, and truth as expressions of God's holiness. Why are these characteristics necessary for any fruitful relationship between people?

2.2 What are we to do when we have broken someone's trust?

2.3 What about when we cannot trust another person?

∽

We are tracing the characteristics God displayed when he reached out to reconcile us to himself. Our thesis is that as we imitate him, as we pursue these same characteristics for ourselves, the people in our lives will expe-rience the benefits of our transformation. The Holy Spirit enables us to do that and, as we follow God, they, too, will grow and flourish.

We have looked at the first characteristic: God's holiness, righteous-ness, and justice. This means we can trust God to be and do what he has said. As we imitate him, people can count on us in the same manner. They can count on us to do what is right and true. It is good news that God is holy. However, by itself this would fail to meet our needs. How could any of us stand before such a God? If this were the end of the story, it would be disastrous. Fortunately for us, it is not. Love is the next characteristic God displayed when he reached out to reconcile us to himself. We have a holy and just God—who loves!

The fact that God is both holy and loving presents a dilemma. How can his love for us, sinful beings that we are, flourish in the face of his holiness? When the holy is mixed with the unholy everything becomes unholy. It seems it would be easier for God if he didn't love us. He would simply judge us all, and we would be history!

But God does love us—profoundly. He has a purpose—a grand idea—that is not just about the here and now. It is about a relationship that will go on forever—between him and us. This is the greatest news imaginable! But how do we know it to be true? The answer to this question will unfold as we proceed through these pages.

3. God is just, but he loves. What dilemma does this present for him?

DEUTERONOMY 4:35–38

You were shown these things so that you might know that the LORD is God; besides him there is no other. From heaven he made you hear his voice to discipline you. On earth he showed you his great fire, and you heard his words from out of the fire. Because he loved your forefathers and chose their descendants after them, he brought you out of Egypt by his Presence and his great strength, to drive out before you nations greater and stronger than you and to bring you into their land to give it to you for your inheritance, as it is today.

> Isaiah records a poignant poem, The Song of the Vineyard, which describes God's frustration. God, described as "the loved one" did everything for his people, but still they failed to bear good fruit.

ISAIAH 5:1–7

I will sing for the one I love, a song about his vineyard: My loved one had a vineyard on a fertile hillside. He dug it up and cleared it of stones and planted it with the choicest vines. He built a watchtower in it and cut out a winepress as well. Then he looked for a crop of good grapes, but it yielded only bad fruit.

"Now you dwellers in Jerusalem and men of Judah, judge between me and my vineyard. What more could have been done for my vineyard than I have done for it? When I looked for good grapes, why did it yield only bad? Now I will tell you what I am going to do to my vineyard: I will take away its hedge, and it will be destroyed; I will break down its wall, and it will be trampled. I will make it a wasteland, neither pruned nor cultivated, and briers and thorns will grow there. I will command the clouds not to rain on it."

The vineyard of the Lord Almighty is the house of Israel, and the men of Judah are the garden of his delight. And he looked for justice, but saw bloodshed; for righteousness, but heard cries of distress.

HOSEA 11:8–9

How can I give you up, Ephraim? How can I hand you over, Israel? How can I treat you like Admah? How can I make you like Zeboiim? My heart is changed within me; all my compassion is aroused. I will not carry out my fierce anger, nor will I turn and devastate Ephraim. For I am God, and not man—the Holy One among you. I will not come in wrath.

EPHESIANS 2:4–7

But because of his great love for us, God, who is rich in mercy, made us alive with Christ even when we were dead in transgressions—it is by grace you have been saved. And God raised us up with Christ and seated us with him in the heavenly realms in Christ Jesus, in order that in the coming ages he might show the incomparable riches of his grace, expressed in his kindness to us in Christ Jesus.

3.1 Summarize God's apparent dilemma.

3.2 How did he handle this as he related to Israel?

3.3 What was the outcome when people spurned his love? Why?

3.4 Is this tension something only God confronts, or is it also a part of our human experience?

3.5 When you are faced with the tension of having to choose between treating people with love and doing what is just in your business, how did you handle this?

๛

B. Love

God loves us. The death and resurrection of Jesus is God's way of re-solving the tension. It allows him to satisfy both his justice and his love. "He himself bore our sins in his body on the tree, so that we might die to sins and live for righteousness . . . " (1 Peter 2:24).

4. Love is a verb. It is expressed in action. The following scriptures describe ways in which God loves. What are they?

DEUTERONOMY 7:7–9

The Lord did not set his affection on you and choose you because you were more numerous than other peoples, for you were the fewest of all peoples. But it was because the Lord loved you and kept the oath he swore to your forefathers that he brought you out with a mighty hand and redeemed you from the land of slavery, from the power of Pharaoh king of Egypt. Know therefore that the Lord your God is God; he is the faithful God, keeping his covenant of love to a thousand generations of those who love him and keep his commands.

> To capture the real meaning of love, we have to strip away layers of popular culture. The Scriptures point to a love that is neither sentimental nor erotic.

PSALM 103:8–13

The Lord is compassionate and gracious, slow to anger, abounding in love. He will not always accuse, nor will he harbor his anger forever; he does not treat us as our sins deserve or repay us according to our iniquities. For as high as the heavens are above the earth, so great is his love for those who fear him; as far as the east is from the west, so far has he removed our transgressions from us. As a father has compassion on his children, so the Lord has compassion on those who fear him.

ISAIAH 63:7–9

I will tell of the kindnesses of the Lord, the deeds for which he is to be praised, according to all the Lord has done for us—yes, the many good things he has done for the house of Israel, according to his compassion and many kindnesses. He said, "Surely they are my people, sons who will not be false to me"; and so he became their Savior. In all their distress he too was distressed, and the angel of his presence saved them. In his love and mercy he redeemed them; he lifted them up and carried them all the days of old.

> The simple phrase, 'For God so loved the world...' would have puzzled an educated pagan. And the notion that the gods care how we treat one another would have been dismissed as patently absurd. *Rodney Stark*

JOHN 3:16

For God so loved the world that he gave his one and only Son, that whoever believes in him shall not perish but have eternal life.

JOHN 17:24–26

Father, I want those you have given me to be with me where I am, and to see my glory, the glory you have given me because you loved me before the creation of the world. Righteous Father, though the world does not know you, I know you, and they know that you have sent me. I have made you known to them, and will continue to make you known in order that the love you have for me may be in them and that I myself may be in them.

ROMANS 8:38–39

For I am convinced that neither death nor life, neither angels nor demons, neither the present nor the future, nor any powers, neither height nor depth, nor anything else in all creation, will be able to separate us from the love of God that is in Christ Jesus our Lord.

1 JOHN 3:1–3

How great is the love the Father has lavished on us, that we should be called children of God! And that is what we are! The reason the world does not know us is that it did not know him. Dear friends, now we are children of God, and what we will be has not yet been made known. But we know that when he appears, we shall be like him, for we shall see him as he is. Everyone who has this hope in him purifies himself, just as he is pure.

4.1 In what ways has God expressed his love to us?

4.2 How have you been impacted by God's love?

5. Jesus said, " . . . love one another. As I have loved you, so must you love one another. By this all men will know that you are my disciples, if you love one another" (John 13:34–35). These are words of such magnitude that they are almost beyond our comprehension. How can we possibly express this kind of love?

MATTHEW 5:43–47

You have heard that it was said, 'Love your neighbor and hate your enemy.' But I tell you: Love your enemies and pray for those who persecute you, that you may be sons of your Father in heaven. He causes his sun to rise on the evil and the good, and sends rain on the righteous and the unrighteous. If you love those who love you, what reward will you get? Are not even the tax collectors doing that? And if you greet only your brothers, what are you doing more than others? Do not even pagans do that?

> Merely trying to act lovingly will lead to despair and to the defeat of love. It will make us angry and hopeless. But taking love itself—God's kind of love—into the depths of our being . . . will, by contrast, enable us to act lovingly to an extent that will be surprising even to ourselves. *Dallas Willard*

MATTHEW 22:37–40

Jesus replied: "'Love the Lord your God with all your heart and with all your soul and with all your mind.' This is the first and greatest commandment. And the second is like it: 'Love your neighbor as your-self.' All the Law and the Prophets hang on these two commandments."

ROMANS 13:8–10

Let no debt remain outstanding, except the continuing debt to love one another, for he who loves his fellowman has fulfilled the law. The commandments, "Do not commit adultery," "Do not murder," "Do not steal," "Do not covet," and whatever other commandment there may be, are summed up in this one rule: "Love your neighbor as yourself." Love does no harm to its neighbor. Therefore love is the fulfillment of the law.

1 CORINTHIANS 13:4–7 (AMPLIFIED)

Love endures long and is patient and kind; love never is envious nor boils over with jealousy; is not boastful or vainglorious, does not display itself haughtily. It is not conceited—arrogant and inflated with pride; it is not rude (unmannerly), and does not act unbecomingly. Love [God's love in us] does not insist on its own rights or its own way, for it is not self-seeking; it is not touchy or fretful or resentful; it takes no account of the evil done to it—pays no attention to a suffered wrong. It does not rejoice at injustice and unrighteousness, but rejoices when right and truth prevail. Love bears up under anything and everything that comes, is ever ready to believe the best of every person, its hopes are fadeless under all circumstances and it endures everything [without weakening].

> Each of us has an unavoidable, crucial choice: Are we going to live for others or for ourselves? The Scriptures teach that this choice will not only determine whether our lives are meaningful or empty, but whether or not the fabric of our society will hold together. *Glenn McMahan and Jim Petersen*

EPHESIANS 5:25–28

Husbands, love your wives, just as Christ loved the church and gave himself up for her to make her holy, cleansing her by the washing with water through the word, and to present her to himself as a radiant church, without stain or wrinkle or any other blemish, but holy and blameless. In this same way, husbands ought to love their wives as their own bodies. He who loves his wife loves himself.

1 PETER 4:7–11

The end of all things is near. Therefore be clear minded and self-controlled so that you can pray. Above all, love each other deeply, because love covers over a multitude of sins. Offer hospitality to one another without grumbling. Each one should use whatever gift he has received to serve others, faithfully administering God's grace in its various forms. If anyone speaks, he should do it as one speaking the very words of God. If anyone serves, he should do it with the strength God provides, so that in all things God may be praised through Jesus Christ. To him be the glory and the power for ever and ever.

> To love at all is to be vulnerable. Love anything, and your heart will certainly be wrung and possibly be broken. If you want to make sure of keeping it intact, you must give your heart to no one, not even to an animal. Wrap it carefully around with hobbies and little luxuries; avoid all entanglements; lock it up safe in the casket or coffin of your selfishness. *C.S. Lewis*

1 JOHN 3:16–17

This is how we know what love is: Jesus Christ laid down his life for us. And we ought to lay down our lives for our brothers. If anyone has material possessions and sees his brother in need but has no pity on him, how can the love of God be in him?

1 JOHN 2:16

For everything in the world—the cravings of sinful man, the lust of his eyes and the boasting of what he has and does—comes not from the Father but from the world.

1 JOHN 3:17–18

If anyone has material possessions and sees his brother in need but has no pity on him, how can the love of God be in him? Dear children, let us not love with words or tongue but with actions and in truth.

1 JOHN 4:16–21

And so we know and rely on the love God has for us. God is love. Whoever lives in love lives in God, and God in him. In this way, love is made complete among us so that we will have confidence on the day of judgment, because in this world we are like him. There is no fear in love. But perfect love drives out fear, because fear has to do with punishment. The one who fears is not made perfect in love. We love because he first loved us. If anyone says, "I love God," yet hates his brother, he is a liar. For anyone who does not love his brother, whom he has seen, cannot love God, whom he has not seen. And he has given us this command: Whoever loves God must also love his brother.

5.1 Love is a verb. It requires action and service. What action does love call for as we relate to:

a) our spouses?

b) our employees or customers?

c) our enemies or critics?

5.2 What does it mean to love a child who has become rebellious?

5.3 What does it mean to love a business colleague who has wronged you?

5.4 Do you have a situation of this nature in your life? Describe it briefly.

✍

C. Humility

Humility is the third of the four characteristics that God displayed as he reconciled us into a relationship with himself.

The incarnation, the act of God becoming a man and living among us, reveals many things about him that we would never have understood otherwise. In it we see the perfection of God's holiness and the extent of his love. But there is more! The incarnation also stands as the greatest demonstration of humility we can ever imagine. Jesus Christ, the creator and sustainer of the universe, came to spend some thirty years in the midst of those who opposed and crucified him. What unbelievable humility! Eugene Peterson translates John 1:14 as follows:

"The Word became flesh and blood and moved into the neighborhood. We saw the glory with our own eyes, the one-of-a-kind glory. Like Father, like Son. Generous inside and out. True from start to finish."

Humility leads us to take the other person seriously. It compels us to get into the other's shoes...moving "into their neighborhood." It is incomprehensible that the creator and Lord of the universe would voluntarily submit to the way we treated him. And yet he did.

Humility, sending his Son, was God's first step toward reconciliation. We can understand the role of humility with this illustration:

6. *Two extraordinary scriptures give us a glimpse into what this submission must have been like. How would you describe such humble submission?*

ISAIAH 53:1–11

Who has believed our message and to whom has the arm of the Lord been revealed? He grew up before him like a tender shoot, and like a root out of dry ground. He had no beauty or majesty to attract us to him, nothing in his appearance that we should desire him. He was despised and rejected by men, a man of sorrows, and familiar with suffering. Like one from whom men hide their faces he was despised, and we esteemed him not.

Surely he took up our infirmities and carried our sorrows, yet we considered him stricken by God, smitten by him, and afflicted. But he was pierced for our transgressions, he was crushed for our iniquities; the punishment that brought us peace was upon him, and by his wounds we are healed. We all, like sheep, have gone astray, each of us has turned to his own way; and the Lord has laid on him the iniquity of us all.

He was oppressed and afflicted, yet he did not open his mouth; he was led like a lamb to the slaughter, and as a sheep before her shearers is silent, so he did not open his mouth. By oppression and judgment he was taken away. And who can speak of his descendants? For he was cut off from the land of the living; for the transgression of my people he was stricken. He was assigned a grave with the wicked, and with the rich in his death, though he had done no violence, nor was any deceit in his mouth.

Yet it was the Lord's will to crush him and cause him to suffer, and though the Lord makes his life a guilt offering, he will see his offspring and prolong his days, and the will of the Lord will prosper in his hand. After the suffering of his soul, he will see the light of life and be satisfied; by his knowledge my righteous servant will justify many, and he will bear their iniquities.

Without humility there can be no true abiding in God's presence or experience of his favor and the power of his spirit. Without it there can be no abiding faith or love or joy or strength. *Andrew Murray*

PHILIPPIANS 2:5–11

Your attitude should be the same as that of Christ Jesus: Who, being in very nature God, did not consider equality with God something to be grasped, but made himself nothing, taking the very nature of a servant, being made in human likeness. And being found in appearance as a man, he humbled himself and became obedient to death—even death on a cross! Therefore God exalted him to the highest place and gave him the name that is above every name, that at the name of Jesus every knee should bow, in heaven and on earth and under the earth, and every tongue confess that Jesus Christ is Lord, to the glory of God the Father.

6.1 What does the model of Jesus teach us about humility?

⤢

Since Jesus is the exact representation of the Father's nature (Hebrews 1:3), it should follow that humility would also characterize the Father. Are we saying God is humble? Or is humility exclusive to the incarnate Christ?

There are passages in the Old Testament where we find evidence that the rule stands. For example, we find God openly pleading with his people to listen to him. He often unashamedly begs people to avoid the consequences of his own justice! The following scriptures are examples.

7. Describe the attitudes God displays in these scriptures?

JEREMIAH 2:4–8

Hear the word of the Lord, O house of Jacob, all you clans of the house of Israel. This is what the Lord says: "What fault did your fathers find in me, that they strayed so far from me? They followed worthless idols and became worthless themselves. They did not ask, 'Where is the Lord, who brought us up out of Egypt and led us through the barren wilderness, through a land of deserts and rifts, a land of drought and darkness, a land where no one travels and no one lives?' I brought you into a fertile land to eat its fruit and rich produce. But you came and defiled my land and made my inheritance detestable. The priests did not ask, 'Where is the Lord?' Those who deal with the law did not know me; the leaders rebelled against me. The prophets prophesied by Baal, following worthless idols."

JEREMIAH 3:19–21

I myself said, "'How gladly would I treat you like sons and give you a desirable land, the most beautiful inheritance of any nation.' I thought you would call me 'Father' and not turn away from following me. But like a woman unfaithful to her husband, so you have been unfaithful to me, O house of Israel," declares the Lord.

> Jesus didn't abandon the law and justice. Yet by his actions he left no doubt that people could come to God in whatever condition and find his love. In this way, Jesus modeled how humility is an essential component for all human relationships. It opens the door to intimacy. *Glenn McMahan*

HOSEA 11:1-8

When Israel was a child, I loved him, and out of Egypt I called my son. But the more I called Israel, the further they went from me. They sacrificed to the Baals and they burned incense to images. It was I who taught Ephraim to walk, taking them by the arms; but they did not realize it was I who healed them. I led them with cords of human kindness, with ties of love; I lifted the yoke from their neck and bent down to feed them. Will they not return to Egypt and will not Assyria rule over them because they refuse to repent? Swords will flash in their cities, will destroy the bars of their gates and put an end to their plans. My people are determined to turn from me. Even if they call to the Most High, he will by no means exalt them. How can I give you up, Ephraim? How can I hand you over, Israel? How can I treat you like Admah? How can I make you like Zeboiim? My heart is changed within me; all my compassion is aroused.

7.1 If God is all powerful, why does he resort to pleading with people? Why doesn't he just do what he wants with them?

⟨§⟩

Some of God's greatest promises are reserved for those who are humble. As we will see, it is as though humility is a prerequisite to any intimacy with him or to his blessing in our lives.

8. What rewards does God promise to the humble?

ISAIAH 57:15

For this is what the high and lofty One says—he who lives forever, whose name is holy: "I live in a high and holy place, but also with him who is contrite and lowly in spirit, to revive the spirit of the lowly and to revive the heart of the contrite."

Jim Collins writes that a great Level 5 executive "builds enduring greatness through a paradoxical combination of personal humility plus professional will." Such a leader, Collins observes:
• Demonstrates a compelling modesty, shuns public adulation, never boasts.
• Acts with calm determination.
• Channels ambition into the company, not the self.
• Looks in the mirror, not out the window; apportions responsibility; never blames other people, external factors, or bad luck.

ISAIAH 66:1–2

This is what the Lord says: "Heaven is my throne, and the earth is my footstool. Where is the house you will build for me? Where will my resting place be? Has not my hand made all these things, and so they came into being?" declares the Lord. "This is the one I esteem: he who is humble and contrite in spirit, and trembles at my word."

DANIEL 10:12

Then he continued, "Do not be afraid, Daniel. Since the first day that you set your mind to gain understanding and to humble yourself before your God, your words were heard, and I have come in response to them."

1 PETER 5:5–7

Young men, in the same way be submissive to those who are older. All of you, clothe yourselves with humility toward one another, because, "God opposes the proud but gives grace to the humble." Humble yourselves, therefore, under God's mighty hand, that he may lift you up in due time. Cast all your anxiety on him because he cares for you.

8.1 Why do you think God rewards the humble?

8.2 Why is humility so important in our relationship with God?

᪅

By examining the qualities God displayed as he reconciled us to himself, we learn how to relate to him—and how to relate to every other person in our lives.

We have identified humility as the third characteristic in which we are to imitate God. "Your attitude should be the same as that of Christ . . ." (Philippians 2:5).

How is this going to work? We live in a society that holds self-promo-tion and self-fulfillment among its highest values. Our marketplace lives by hard competition. One-liners like, "You owe it to yourself to achieve your full potential" and "Don't let 'em see you sweat," don't exactly lead to hu-mility! Humility is a stranger in today's culture—we view it as a weakness. Some of our problems with humility probably have to do with our under-standing—or misunderstanding—of what it is.

9. In the light of the following scriptures, how would you de-fine humility?

NUMBERS 12:3
     Now Moses was a very humble man, more humble than anyone else on the face of the earth.

> Moses was one of the most powerful leaders in human history. He was the catalyst to the emancipation of over a million people from slavery, and he led them for forty years as nomads in the desert. How do you fit leadership and humility together?

JOHN 3:27-30
     To this John replied, "A man can receive only what is given him from heaven. You yourselves can testify that I said, 'I am not the Christ but am sent ahead of him.' The bride belongs to the bridegroom. The friend who attends the bridegroom waits and listens for him, and is full of joy when he hears the bridegroom's voice. That joy is mine, and it is now complete. He must become greater; I must become less."

2 CORINTHIANS 12:7-12
     To keep me from becoming conceited because of these surpassingly great rev-elations, there was given me a thorn in my flesh, a messenger of Satan, to torment me. Three times I pleaded with the Lord to take it away from me. But he said to me, "My grace is sufficient for you, for my power is made perfect in weakness." There-fore I will boast all the more gladly about my weaknesses, so that Christ's power may rest on me. That is why, for Christ's sake, I delight in weaknesses, in insults, in hardships, in persecutions, in difficulties. For when I am weak, then I am strong. I have made a fool of myself, but you drove me to it. I ought to have been commend-ed by you, for I am not in the least inferior to the "super-apostles," even though I am nothing. The things that mark an apostle—signs, wonders and miracles—were done among you with great perseverance.

Only he who lives by the forgiveness of his sin in Jesus Christ will rightly think little of himself. *Dietrich Bonhoeffer*

PHILIPPIANS 2:1–5

If you have any encouragement from being united with Christ, if any comfort from his love, if any fellowship with the Spirit, if any tenderness and compassion, then make my joy complete by being like-minded, having the same love, being one in spirit and purpose. Do nothing out of selfish ambition or vain conceit, but in humility consider others better than yourselves. Each of you should look not only to your own interests, but also to the interests of others. Your attitude should be the same as that of Christ Jesus. . . .

COLOSSIANS 3:12–13

Therefore, as God's chosen people, holy and dearly loved, clothe yourselves with compassion, kindness, humility, gentleness and patience. Bear with each other and forgive whatever grievances you may have against one another. Forgive as the Lord forgave you.

I challenge you to find a sin that does not spill out of pride. Envy. Anger. Greed. Lust. Ambition. Ingratitude. You name it. They all find their root here, in this 'Mother and Queen of all vices,' as Gregory the Great put it. Pride is The Sin, the plant from which all other sins are mere offshoots.

JAMES 3:13–4:10

Who is wise and understanding among you? Let him show it by his good life, by deeds done in the humility that comes from wisdom. But if you harbor bitter envy and selfish ambition in your hearts, do not boast about it or deny the truth. Such "wisdom" does not come down from heaven but is earthly, unspiritual, of the devil. For where you have envy and selfish ambition, there you find disorder and every evil practice. But the wisdom that comes from heaven is first of all pure; then peace-loving, considerate, submissive, full of mercy and good fruit, impartial and sincere. Peacemakers who sow in peace raise a harvest of righteousness. What causes fights and quarrels among you? Don't they come from your desires that battle within you? You want something but don't get it. You kill and covet, but you cannot have what you want. You quarrel and fight. You do not have, because you do not ask God. When you ask, you do not receive, because you ask with wrong motives, that you may spend what you get on your pleasures. You adulterous people, don't you know that friendship with the world is hatred toward God? Anyone who chooses to be a friend of the world becomes an enemy of God. Or do you think Scripture says without reason that the spirit he caused to live in us envies intensely? But he gives us more grace. That is why Scripture says: "God opposes the proud but gives grace to the humble." Submit yourselves, then, to God. Resist the devil, and he will flee from you. Come near to God and he will come near to you. Wash your hands, you sinners, and purify your hearts, you double-minded.

Grieve, mourn and wail. Change your laughter to mourning and your joy to gloom. Humble yourselves before the Lord, and he will lift you up.

> A case study: A woman has joined a previously all-male executive team. The men on the team find it difficult to think of her as a peer. They relate to her as an office girl, secretary, or as their travel agent. What guidance can this woman take from this subject of humility that would help her develop peer relationships with the others? Is humility incompatible with her need to establish respect among the others on the team?

9.1 What is humility?

9.2 Why is humility essential in relating to the people in our lives?

9.3 What could be the effect of humility in the workplace?

◦◦

Often, humility is not easy to see in others or recognize even in oneself. Pride is its opposite. And pride is easy to spot, especially in someone else! Think of a current or past personal conflict: Whether it's a temporary chill between you and your spouse or a full-blown war between you and a business associate, you can be sure of one thing: pride is at the core of it!

"Pride only breeds quarrels, but wisdom is found in those who take advice" (Proverbs 13:10).

10. When a conflict erupts, we need to pursue a godly resolution. But how are we to do this? What do these scriptures tell us?

EPHESIANS 4:2
Be completely humble and gentle; be patient, bearing with one another in love.

JAMES 1:19–25
My dear brothers, take note of this: Everyone should be quick to listen, slow to speak and slow to become angry, for man's anger does not bring about the righteous life that God desires. Therefore, get rid of all moral filth and the evil that is so

prevalent and humbly accept the word planted in you, which can save you. Do not merely listen to the word, and so deceive yourselves. Do what it says. Anyone who listens to the word but does not do what it says is like a man who looks at his face in a mirror and, after looking at himself, goes away and immediately forgets what he looks like. But the man who looks intently into the perfect law that gives freedom, and continues to do this, not forgetting what he has heard, but doing it—he will be blessed in what he does.

Seek first to understand, then to be understood. *Steven Covey*

10.1 What would happen to conflict if pride were eliminated?

10.2 How would applying the principles in these scriptures affect the conflict?

10.3 Did you notice the relationship between humility and listening? What's the connection?

<del>&</del>

Swiss psychiatrist and author, Paul Tournier, has said that people have three basic needs: to be listened to; to be understood; to be taken seriously. We are ready to resolve a conflict when we are ready to do these three things. This is where humility comes in. It takes humility to listen in this way. It takes humility to set our own opinions aside long enough to understand and to seriously consider the other's point of view. Humility creates the necessary space to resolve the differences and conflicts.

D. Forgiveness

Forgiveness is the fourth characteristic God expressed when he reconciled us to himself. As we begin our discussion about forgiveness, let's review what we've already discovered.

First, God is holy; we are not. This difference separates us from him. Justice demands judgment, but we are spared by his love for us. Christ humbled himself, came to us as a servant, obedient to the point of death—all this in order to rightly forgive us. "In him we have redemption through his blood, the *forgiveness of sins* . . . " (Ephesians 1:7, italics added). He did all this to give us a way to be reconciled to him.

The very idea of forgiveness has its origins in the message of the Bible. In cultures where the news of Jesus Christ has not penetrated, we find that the power of forgiveness is usually not present. In its place we find attitudes such as revenge, defending one's honor, the need to save face whatever the cost, or smoldering denial. These are harsh, even frightening alternatives.

Forgiveness should be a visible aspect of societies fertilized by the Gospel. Forgiveness is a theme which runs from Genesis to Revelation, but we struggle with it. Perhaps that is because it is contrary to our broken nature to truly forgive. So we need to learn from God what it means to forgive.

11. What do the following scriptures tell us about God's forgiveness?

2 CHRONICLES 7:13–14
    When I shut up the heavens so that there is no rain, or command locusts to devour the land or send a plague among my people, if my people, who are called by my name, will humble themselves and pray and seek my face and turn from their wicked ways, then will I hear from heaven and will forgive their sin and will heal their land.

> Classical philosophers regarded mercy and pity as pathological emotions—defects of character to be avoided by all rational men. Since mercy involves providing unearned help or relief, it was contrary to justice. This was the moral climate in which Christianity taught that mercy is one of the primary virtues—that a merciful God requires humans to be merciful. *Rodney Stark*

PSALM 32:1–5
    Blessed is he whose transgressions are forgiven, whose sins are covered. Blessed is the man whose sin the Lord does not count against him and in whose spirit is no deceit. When I kept silent, my bones wasted away through my groaning all day long. For day and night your hand was heavy upon me; my strength was sapped as in the heat of summer. Then I acknowledged my sin to you and did not cover up my iniquity. I said, "I will confess my transgressions to the Lord"—and you forgave the guilt of my sin.

> Forgiveness is God's invention for coming to terms with a world in which, despite their best intentions, people are unfair to each other and hurt each other deeply. Forgiveness seems almost unnatural. . . . Our sense of fairness tells us that people should pay for the wrong they do. But forgiveness is love's power to break nature's rule. *Lewis Smedes*

PSALM 103:8–13

The Lord is compassionate and gracious, slow to anger, abounding in love. He will not always accuse, nor will he harbor his anger forever; he does not treat us as our sins deserve or repay us according to our iniquities. For as high as the heavens are above the earth, so great is his love for those who fear him; as far as the east is from the west, so far has he removed our transgressions from us. As a father has compassion on his children, so the Lord has compassion on those who fear him. . . .

ISAIAH 43:25

I, even I, am he who blots out your transgressions, for my own sake, and remembers your sins no more.

JEREMIAH 5:7

Why should I forgive you? Your children have forsaken me and sworn by gods that are not gods. I supplied all their needs, yet they committed adultery and thronged to the houses of prostitutes.

JEREMIAH 36:3

Perhaps when the people of Judah hear about every disaster I plan to inflict on them, each of them will turn from his wicked way; then I will forgive their wickedness and their sin.

> The Parable of the Prodigal Son in Luke 15:11–32 could better be called the Parable of the Forgiving Father. The son had insulted and shamed his father by asking for his money while the father was still alive. By doing this, he broke social norms and became a rebel who dishonored his father. When the son slunk home and applied to be hired, we read the familiar words—"while he was still a long way off, his father saw him and was filled with compassion for him; he ran to his son, threw his arms around him and kissed him."

MARK 2:6–11

Now some teachers of the law were sitting there, thinking to themselves, "Why does this fellow talk like that? He's blaspheming! Who can forgive sins but God alone?" Immediately Jesus knew in his spirit that this was what they were thinking in their hearts, and he said to them, "Why are you thinking these things? Which is easier: to say to the paralytic, 'Your sins are forgiven,' or to say, 'Get up, take your mat and walk'? But that you may know that the Son of Man has authority on earth to forgive sins. . . ." He said to the paralytic, "I tell you, get up, take your mat and go home."

ACTS 26:15–18

"Then I asked, 'Who are you, Lord?'

"'I am Jesus, whom you are persecuting,' the Lord replied. 'Now get up and stand on your feet. I have appeared to you to appoint you as a servant and as a witness of what you have seen of me and what I will show you. I will rescue you from your own people and from the Gentiles. I am sending you to them to open their eyes and turn them from darkness to light, and from the power of Satan to God, so that they may receive forgiveness of sins and a place among those who are sanctified by faith in me.'"

HEBREWS 9:22

In fact, the law requires that nearly everything be cleansed with blood, and without the shedding of blood there is no forgiveness.

11.1 Based on these passages, what is forgiveness?

11.2 What does it mean to be forgiven by God?

11.3 What are the effects of forgiveness on the forgiven? For the forgiver?

⁓

This whole idea of forgiveness is immensely powerful. But it goes against the grain of our broken human nature. It offends our sense of fairness. But when we imitate God in this way, the world can't help but notice.

12. Jesus addresses this matter of forgiveness in the following parable. It is a disturbing, difficult little story. What do you make of it? Who is the king? Who owes 10,000 talents? Who is the fellow servant?

(Note: A talent weighs about 1,000 pounds. So, the debt was about 1,000,000 pounds of silver. A denarius equals the daily wage of a laborer at that time.)

MATTHEW 18:21–35

Then Peter came to Jesus and asked, "Lord, how many times shall I forgive my brother when he sins against me? Up to seven times?"

Jesus answered, "I tell you, not seven times, but seventy-seven times. Therefore, the kingdom of heaven is like a king who wanted to settle accounts with his servants. As he began the settlement, a man who owed him ten thousand talents was brought to him. Since he was not able to pay, the master ordered that he and his wife and his children and all that he had be sold to repay the debt. The servant fell on his knees before him. 'Be patient with me,' he begged, 'and I will pay back everything.' The servant's master took pity on him, canceled the debt and let him go. But when that servant went out, he found one of his fellow servants who owed him a hundred denarii. He grabbed him and began to choke him. 'Pay back what you owe me!' he demanded. His fellow servant fell to his knees and begged him, 'Be patient with me, and I will pay you back.' But he refused. Instead, he went off and had the man thrown into prison until he could pay the debt. When the other servants saw what had happened, they were greatly distressed and went and told their master everything that had happened. Then the master called the servant in. 'You wicked servant,' he said, 'I canceled all that debt of yours because you begged me to. Shouldn't you have had mercy on your fellow servant just as I had on you?' In anger his master turned him over to the jailers to be tortured, until he should pay back all he owed. This is how my heavenly Father will treat each of you unless you forgive your brother from your heart."

> It would be incomprehensible to be the recipient of God's forgiveness and not, in turn, forgive others. It would mean we really understood nothing at all of what God has done for us.

12.1 Why do you think the servant was so unforgiving toward his fellow servant, even after his master pardoned him?

12.2 How do you understand the outcome of the story?

⁓

What could be greater than to be forgiven by God—to know that there are absolutely no judgments against us? Realizing this alters our whole outlook on life!

Jesus' story teaches us that forgiven people will, in turn, be forgiving. That sounds obvious! It looks simple, that is, until we try to put it into practice. Then we run into all sorts of problems. Am I to forgive every offense? What does that mean? Does forgiving mean forgetting? Am I to forget every wrong and continue as if nothing happened?

What am I to do when a person piles one offense upon another, showing no remorse and making no effort to change? What about the person who refuses to acknowledge his or her wrong action? Work in the kingdom of God has multiple objectives; it's not just about the bottom line, it's about revealing God to those in our sphere of influence. So, forgiveness plays an important role in the purposes of God in the workplace. The questions continue.

What is forgiveness? When have I truly forgiven someone? Is it a one-way or a two-way street? Are there times when it would be wrong for me to forgive? These questions make us realize that forgiving is not simple.

13. Trace how forgiveness plays out in the following scriptures.

MATTHEW 18:21–22

Then Peter came to Jesus and asked, "Lord, how many times shall I forgive my brother when he sins against me? Up to seven times?" Jesus answered, "I tell you, not seven times, but seventy-seven times."

> Forgiveness is a choice, a decision to release someone from a debt. You no longer feel like the person owes you, and you decide that you will not try to even the score. *Whiteman & Bartlett*

LUKE 6:37

Do not judge, and you will not be judged. Do not condemn, and you will not be condemned. Forgive, and you will be forgiven.

LUKE 23:33–34A

When they came to the place called the Skull, there they crucified him, along with the criminals—one on his right, the other on his left. Jesus said, "Father, forgive them, for they do not know what they are doing. . . ."

> Only a free person can choose to live with an uneven score. Only free people can choose to start over with someone who has hurt them. Only a free person can live with accounts unsettled. Only a free person can heal the memory of hurt and hate. *Lewis Smedes*

ROMANS 12:14–21

Bless those who persecute you; bless and do not curse. Rejoice with those who rejoice; mourn with those who mourn. Live in harmony with one another. Do not be proud, but be willing to associate with people of low position. Do not be conceited. Do not repay anyone evil for evil. Be careful to do what is right in the eyes of everybody. If it is possible, as far as it depends on you, live at peace with everyone. Do not take revenge, my friends, but leave room for God's wrath, for it is written: "It is mine to avenge; I will repay," says the Lord. On the contrary: "If your enemy is hungry, feed him; if he is thirsty, give him something to drink. In doing this, you will heap burning coals on his head."

> The person who chooses to forgive acts contrary to any natural inclinations, for immediate and personal justice is imitating Jesus' response to the unjust treatment he endured. . . . Personal definitions of fairness are set aside. In fact, self is set aside altogether. The focus becomes Christ. However real the offenses or injustices against us, however justified our hurt, we must view it all from the cross-beams of Calvary. True forgiveness rises from a deep-rooted trust in Jesus Christ and in the values of his kingdom.
> *Kathy E. Dahlen*

2 CORINTHIANS 2:7–11

Now instead, you ought to forgive and comfort him, so that he will not be overwhelmed by excessive sorrow. I urge you, therefore, to reaffirm your love for him. The reason I wrote you was to see if you would stand the test and be obedient in everything. If you forgive anyone, I also forgive him. And what I have forgiven—if there was anything to forgive—I have forgiven in the sight of Christ for your sake, in order that Satan might not outwit us. For we are not unaware of his schemes.

EPHESIANS 4:31–5:2

Get rid of all bitterness, rage and anger, brawling and slander, along with every form of malice. Be kind and compassionate to one another, forgiving each other, just as in Christ God forgave you. Be imitators of God, therefore, as dearly loved children and live a life of love, just as Christ loved us and gave himself up for us as a fragrant offering and sacrifice to God.

COLOSSIANS 3:12–14

Therefore, as God's chosen people, holy and dearly loved, clothe yourselves with compassion, kindness, humility, gentleness and patience. Bear with each other and forgive whatever grievances you may have against one another. Forgive as the Lord forgave you. And over all these virtues put on love, which binds them all together in perfect unity.

13.1 Is forgiveness conditional upon the other person's remorse and repentance?

13.2 We are commanded to forgive in all situations. So, what do we do with the pain and loss that result from an injustice? And what is God's part?

13.3 Imagine that a business colleague has defrauded you. Should you continue to pursue business dealings with this person? Explain.

14. What if I realized that I'm the offending party, the one who needs forgiveness? What do I do?

PSALM 51:1–12

Have mercy on me, O God, according to your unfailing love; according to your great compassion blot out my transgressions. Wash away all my iniquity and cleanse me from my sin. For I know my transgressions, and my sin is always before me. Against you, you only, have I sinned and done what is evil in your sight, so that you are proved right when you speak and justified when you judge. Surely I was sinful at birth, sinful from the time my mother conceived me. Surely you desire truth in the inner parts; you teach me wisdom in the inmost place.

Cleanse me with hyssop, and I will be clean; wash me, and I will be whiter than snow. Let me hear joy and gladness; let the bones you have crushed rejoice. Hide your face from my sins and blot out all my iniquity.

Create in me a pure heart, O God, and renew a steadfast spirit within me. Do not cast me from your presence or take your Holy Spirit from me. Restore to me the joy of your salvation and grant me a willing spirit, to sustain me.

> Forgiveness . . . takes a spirit of humility, requires hard work, needs time, requires an open spirit, involves a decision, and is a process.
> *Whiteman & Bartlett*

MATTHEW 5:23–24

Therefore, if you are offering your gift at the altar and there remember that your brother has something against you, leave your gift there in front of the altar. First go and be reconciled to your brother; then come and offer your gift.

2 CORINTHIANS 7:10–11

Godly sorrow brings repentance that leads to salvation and leaves no regret, but worldly sorrow brings death. See what this godly sorrow has produced in you: what earnestness, what eagerness to clear yourselves, what indignation, what alarm, what longing, what concern, what readiness to see justice done. At every point you have proved yourselves to be innocent in this matter.

14.1 What do I need to do in order to seek forgiveness from another person? How do I show my sincerity?

ख़

F. The Path to Reconciliation

We have looked at four characteristics God displayed toward us as he opened the path to our reconciliation. We have also seen how these same qualities should be instilled in us as we relate to the people in our lives. Our relationships with others should be a visual expression of what God has done in our hearts.

God took the initiative to open the way to our reconciliation. "For if, when we were God's enemies, we were reconciled to him through the death of his Son, how much more, having been reconciled, shall we be saved by his life?" (Romans 5:10).

It follows now that we are to imitate what we have seen and experienced. We are to offer the same kind of path in relating to others. We are to live as reconcilers. "Let us therefore make every effort to do what leads to peace and to mutual edification" (Romans 14:19). It's our move.

In practical terms, what does that mean? How do I make these qualities a part of my lifestyle?

15. *Reflect on the following scripture.*

2 CORINTHIANS 5:17–21

Therefore, if anyone is in Christ, he is a new creation; the old has gone, the new has come! All this is from God, who reconciled us to himself through Christ and gave us the ministry of reconciliation: that God was reconciling the world to himself in Christ, not counting men's sins against them. And he has committed to us the message of reconciliation. We are therefore Christ's ambassadors, as though God were making his appeal through us. We implore you on Christ's behalf: Be reconciled to God. God made him who had no sin to be sin for us, so that in him we might become the righteousness of God.

15.1 Ask yourself these questions about the most important person in your life?

- **Integrity: Does he/she trust me?**
- **Love: Do I consistently act to strengthen and encourage this person?**
- **Humility: Do I make it easy for him/her to talk to me about issues in our relationship? Do I listen?**
- **Forgiveness: Are there tensions or frictions between us?**

15.2 What do your answers to these questions tell you about the quality of this relationship?

15.3 Suppose you took it upon yourself to give special attention to this relationship, to put these four virtues into practice over the next few months. What would be some likely outcomes?

15.4 Now apply these same virtues to another, less intimate relationship. Think of a friend or business associate with whom you interact constantly. There is conflict. Ask yourself:

- **Integrity: Is there trust between us?**
- **Love: Am I interested in this person's life—his/her well-being? Am I looking out for his/her good and serving?**
- **Humility: Do we compete with each other?**
- **Forgiveness: Does he/she feel comfortable talking to me about his/her mistakes? About my mistakes?**

15.5 Suppose you made the first moves to improve this relationship. Where would you start?

15.6 How do you think such initiatives on your part might eventually affect this relationship?

⊷

It would be easy to come to this point in our discussion and feel over-whelmed. The ideas we are talking about are so challenging and can be so far from the realities of our everyday experience that we might find it hard to relate to them. We could be tempted to write them off as being unrealis-tic, beyond reach.

But the question is not, do I find these ideas doable? The question is, are they biblical? If we agree they are—that this is how God really wants us to live—then there has to be a way to do it.

The Christian life is not a self-help project. We do not get a make-over and come out looking like Jesus. Rather, we are transformed, day by day, by the Holy Spirit who was sent to live in us for this very purpose. The great adventure in life is to experience how he transforms us into people we could never hope to be if we had to do it on our own.

16. How does the Holy Spirit help me attain the virtues we have examined? What does he leave for me to do?

JOHN 14:25–26

All this I have spoken while still with you. But the Counselor, the Holy Spirit, whom the Father will send in my name, will teach you all things and will remind you of everything I have said to you.

> He saves us by realistic restoration of our heart to God, and then dwelling there with his Father through the distinctively divine Spirit. The heart thus renovated and inhabited is the only real hope of humanity on earth.
> *Dallas Willard*

JOHN 16:12–15

I have much more to say to you, more than you can now bear. But when he, the Spirit of truth, comes, he will guide you into all truth. He will not speak on his own; he will speak only what he hears, and he will tell you what is yet to come. He will bring glory to me by taking from what is mine and making it known to you. All that belongs to the Father is mine. That is why I said the Spirit will take from what is mine and make it known to you.

2 CORINTHIANS 3:17–18

Now the Lord is the Spirit, and where the Spirit of the Lord is, there is freedom. And we, who with unveiled faces all reflect the Lord's glory, are being transformed into his likeness with ever-increasing glory, which comes from the Lord, who is the Spirit.

> In the last analysis the remedy to the human situation must come . . . from the impact upon the human mind and will of the Good News of Jesus Christ under the influence of the Holy Spirit. The human mind and will must be transformed through interaction with thoughts and feelings deriving from the Word and the Spirit. *Dallas Willard*

GALATIANS 5:16–26

So I say, live by the Spirit, and you will not gratify the desires of the sinful nature. For the sinful nature desires what is contrary to the Spirit, and the Spirit what is contrary to the sinful nature. They are in conflict with each other, so that you do not do what you want. But if you are led by the Spirit, you are not under law.

The acts of the sinful nature are obvious: sexual immorality, impurity and debauchery; idolatry and witchcraft; hatred, discord, jealousy, fits of rage, selfish ambition, dissensions, factions and envy; drunkenness, orgies, and the like. I warn you, as I did before, that those who live like this will not inherit the kingdom of God.

But the fruit of the Spirit is love, joy, peace, patience, kindness, goodness, faithfulness, gentleness and self-control. Against such things there is no law. Those who belong to Christ Jesus have crucified the sinful nature with its passions and desires. Since we live by the Spirit, let us keep in step with the Spirit. Let us not become conceited, provoking and envying each other.

EPHESIANS 3:14–19

For this reason I kneel before the Father, from whom his whole family in heaven and on earth derives its name. I pray that out of his glorious riches he may strengthen you with power through his Spirit in your inner being, so that Christ may dwell in your hearts through faith. And I pray that you, being rooted and established in love, may have power, together with all the saints, to grasp how wide and long and high and deep is the love of Christ, and to know this love that surpasses knowledge—that you may be filled to the measure of all the fullness of God.

PHILIPPIANS 2:12–13

Therefore, my dear friends, as you have always obeyed—not only in my presence, but now much more in my absence—continue to work out your salvation with fear and trembling, for it is God who works in you to will and to act according to his good purpose.

16.1 What is the Holy Spirit's role and purpose in our transformation?

16.2 What is the place of prayer in this process?

$\backsim$

We have defined what it is to be like Christ. To imitate him is indeed the goal. The Apostle Paul summarized his life's purpose in these terms: "I want to know Christ and the power of his resurrection and the fellowship of sharing in his sufferings, becoming like him . . ." (Philippians 3:10).

We have been addressing this topic on the individual level—we need to imitate God in order to relate rightly with others. Each one of us is responsible for our own attitudes and actions. No one can do that for us. But in practice, becoming like Christ cannot happen in isolation. It only grows in the soil of relationships, of community with others; "until we all reach unity in the faith and in the knowledge of the Son of God and become mature, attaining to the whole measure of the fullness of Christ" (Ephesians 4:13). To be like Christ is something we achieve together.

Such interdependence with others is a reflection of the way we are made. It comes out of being created in God's image! This is the subject we'll be addressing in the next section. Here we will explore the idea that God is relational and, therefore, so are we.

SECTION NOTES

SECTION 2
CREATED FOR COMMUNITY

God is relational. He has created us to live in relationship, in community, with himself and with one another. Believe it or not, the first model of such a community is God himself! He exists in trinity: as Father, Son, and Holy Spirit. How can three be one—or one be three? God may not fit neatly within our categories, but the interactive workings of the three are clear enough.

At the very beginning of the story, we see the Father creating the heavens and the earth . . . the Spirit hovering over the waters . . . the Son "through whom God made the universe" (Genesis 1:1–2 and Hebrews 1:2). All three persons are engaged in perfect unity. Again, God said on the sixth day, "Let us make man in our image, in our likeness. . . ."

17. What do the following scriptures reveal to us about how the three persons within God live in relationship and work together?

LUKE 3:21–22

When all the people were being baptized, Jesus was baptized too. And as he was praying, heaven was opened and the Holy Spirit descended on him in bodily form like a dove. And a voice came from heaven: "You are my Son, whom I love; with you I am well pleased."

JOHN 14:16–17

And I will ask the Father, and he will give you another Counselor to be with you forever— the Spirit of truth. The world cannot accept him, because it neither sees him nor knows him. But you know him, for he lives with you and will be in you.

The Bible teaches that we are not autonomous individuals. Instead, we are created in the image of the one who in his very essence is a community of being—that is, the Trinity. God's very nature is reciprocal love and communication among the persons of the Trinity. We were created as inherently communal beings. . . . *Charles Colson*

JOHN 16:12–15

I have much more to say to you, more than you can now bear. But when he, the Spirit of truth, comes, he will guide you into all truth. He will not speak on his own; he will speak only what he hears, and he will tell you what is yet to come. He will bring glory to me by taking from what is mine and making it known to you. All that belongs to the Father is mine. That is why I said the Spirit will take from what is mine and make it known to you.

ACTS 1:7–8

He said to them: "It is not for you to know the times or dates the Father has set by his own authority. But you will receive power when the Holy Spirit comes on you; and you will be my witnesses in Jerusalem, and in all Judea and Samaria, and to the ends of the earth."

ACTS 2:38–39

Peter replied, "Repent and be baptized, every one of you, in the name of Jesus Christ for the forgiveness of your sins. And you will receive the gift of the Holy Spirit. The promise is for you and your children and for all who are far off—for all whom the Lord our God will call."

ROMANS 15:16–20

. . . to be a minister of Christ Jesus to the Gentiles with the priestly duty of proclaiming the gospel of God, so that the Gentiles might become an offering acceptable to God, sanctified by the Holy Spirit. Therefore I glory in Christ Jesus in my service to God. I will not venture to speak of anything except what Christ has accomplished through me in leading the Gentiles to obey God by what I have said and done— by the power of signs and miracles, through the power of the Spirit. So from Jerusalem all the way around to Illyricum, I have fully proclaimed the gospel of Christ. It has always been my ambition to preach the gospel where Christ was not known, so that I would not be building on someone else's foundation.

If God is not solitary and exists always in relation, there can be no talk of God that does not involve love. Love unites Father, Son, and Holy Spirit; love brings God into relation with the world, and by love human beings cleave to God. *Robert Wilken*

EPHESIANS 4:2–6

Be completely humble and gentle; be patient, bearing with one another in love. Make every effort to keep the unity of the Spirit through the bond of peace. There is one body and one Spirit—just as you were called to one hope when you were called— one Lord, one faith, one baptism; one God and Father of all, who is over all and through all and in all.

TITUS 3:4–7

But when the kindness and love of God our Savior appeared, he saved us, not because of righteous things we had done, but because of his mercy. He saved us through the washing of rebirth and renewal by the Holy Spirit, whom he poured out on us generously through Jesus Christ our Savior, so that, having been justified by his grace, we might become heirs having the hope of eternal life.

17.1 Here we have the ideal of teamwork. It is organic and relational. And it is teamwork for our benefit. What stands out to you as the most powerful characteristics of the Trinity?

17.2 How should the relational nature of the Trinity shape human relationships?

～⑤

Next we discover that God invites us to collaborate with him. In Book 2, we looked at God's investment in our design and at what it means to be "in his image." Again, in the very first chapter of Genesis, God says:

"Let us make man in our image, in our likeness, and let them rule over the fish of the sea and the birds of the air, over the livestock, over all the earth, and over all the creatures that move along the ground." So God created man in his own image, in the image of God he created him; male and female he created them. God blessed them and said to them, "Be fruitful and increase in number; fill the earth and subdue it. Rule over the fish of the sea and the birds of the air and over every living creature that moves on the ground" (Genesis 1:26–28).

The Trinity helps us understand our own design. God, in himself, is relational, and he has fashioned us accordingly.

18. How do the following scriptures amplify God's deep desire to relate to us?

GENESIS 3:8-10

Then the man and his wife heard the sound of the Lord God as he was walking in the garden in the cool of the day, and they hid from the Lord God among the trees of the garden. But the Lord God called to the man, "Where are you?" He answered, "I heard you in the garden, and I was afraid because I was naked; so I hid."

EXODUS 6:7

I will take you as my own people, and I will be your God. Then you will know that I am the Lord your God, who brought you out from under the yoke of the Egyptians.

EXODUS 19:4–6A

You yourselves have seen what I did to Egypt, and how I carried you on eagles' wings and brought you to myself. Now if you obey me fully and keep my covenant, then out of all nations you will be my treasured possession. Although the whole earth is mine, you will be for me a kingdom of priests and a holy nation.

Almost a dozen times in the Old Testament, God declares his intent—"They will be my people and I will be their God."

JOHN 15:9–17

As the Father has loved me, so have I loved you. Now remain in my love. If you obey my commands, you will remain in my love, just as I have obeyed my Father's commands and remain in his love. I have told you this so that my joy may be in you and that your joy may be complete. My command is this: Love each other as I have loved you. Greater love has no one than this, that he lay down his life for his friends. You are my friends if you do what I command. I no longer call you servants, because a servant does not know his master's business. Instead, I have called you friends, for everything that I learned from my Father I have made known to you. You did not choose me, but I chose you and appointed you to go and bear fruit—fruit that will last. Then the Father will give you whatever you ask in my name. This is my command: Love each other.

JOHN 17:19–23

For them I sanctify myself, that they too may be truly sanctified. My prayer is not for them alone. I pray also for those who will believe in me through their message, that all of them may be one, Father, just as you are in me and I am in you. May they also be in us so that the world may believe that you have sent me. I have given them the glory that you gave me, that they may be one as we are one: I in them and you in me. May they be brought to complete unity to let the world know that you sent me and have loved them even as you have loved me.

1 PETER 2:9

But you are a chosen people, a royal priesthood, a holy nation, a people belonging to God, that you may declare the praises of him who called you out of darkness into his wonderful light.

REVELATION 21:3–4

And I heard a loud voice from the throne saying, "Now the dwelling of God is with men, and he will live with them. They will be his people, and God himself will be with them and be their God. He will wipe every tear from their eyes. There will be no more death or mourning or crying or pain, for the old order of things has passed away."

18.1 From these scriptures, how would you describe the kind of relationship God wants to have with us today? What about in eternity?

∽

As our next focus, we will look at the fact that we are incomplete without community. As human beings made in God's image, we were born to be in relationship with others. We depend upon others for so much, from meeting our daily material necessities to giving us a sense of identity. Personality is shaped and character is developed as we live life together. Indeed, we often assess the quality of our lives by the strength of our relationships. The following scriptures develop this idea.

19. *What are the benefits of living in community?*

GENESIS 2:18–23

The Lord God said, "It is not good for the man to be alone. I will make a helper suitable for him." Now the Lord God had formed out of the ground all the beasts of the field and all the birds of the air. He brought them to the man to see what he would name them; and whatever the man called each living creature, that was its name. So the man gave names to all the livestock, the birds of the air and all the beasts of the field.

But for Adam no suitable helper was found. So the Lord God caused the man to fall into a deep sleep; and while he was sleeping, he took one of the man's ribs and closed up the place with flesh. Then the Lord God made a woman from the rib he had taken out of the man, and he brought her to the man. The man said, "This is now bone of my bones and flesh of my flesh; she shall be called 'woman,' for she was taken out of man."

> How beautiful, how grand and liberating this experience is, when people learn to help each other. It is impossible to overemphasize the immense needs humans have to be really listened to, to be taken seriously, to be understood. *Paul Tournier*

ECCLESIASTES 4:8–12

There was a man all alone; he had neither son nor brother. There was no end to his toil, yet his eyes were not content with his wealth. "For whom am I toiling," he asked, "and why am I depriving myself of enjoyment?" This too is meaningless—a miserable business! Two are better than one, because they have a good return for their work: If one falls down, his friend can help him up. But pity the man who falls and has no one to help him up! Also, if two lie down together, they will keep warm. But how can one keep warm alone? Though one may be overpowered, two can defend themselves. A cord of three strands is not quickly broken.

Judges 18 captures a sad episode in the time before Israel had a king. It tells of the massacre by the Danites of a peaceful and unsuspecting people. "There was no one to rescue them because they lived a long way from Sidon and had no relationship with anyone else."

1 CORINTHIANS 12:12–19

The body is a unit, though it is made up of many parts; and though all its parts are many, they form one body. So it is with Christ. For we were all baptized by one Spirit into one body—whether Jews or Greeks, slave or free—and we were all given the one Spirit to drink.

Now the body is not made up of one part but of many. If the foot should say, "Because I am not a hand, I do not belong to the body," it would not for that reason cease to be part of the body. And if the ear should say, "Because I am not an eye, I do not belong to the body," it would not for that reason cease to be part of the body. If the whole body were an eye, where would the sense of hearing be? If the whole body were an ear, where would the sense of smell be? But in fact God has arranged the parts in the body, every one of them, just as he wanted them to be. If they were all one part, where would the body be?

It was the capacity for intimate relationships that predicted flourishing in all aspects of these men's lives. *George Vaillant, director of the Grant Study, which, beginning in 1938, followed the lives of 268 Harvard graduates.*

HEBREWS 10:24–25

And let us consider how we may spur one another on toward love and good deeds. Let us not give up meeting together, as some are in the habit of doing, but let us encourage one another—and all the more as you see the Day approaching.

1 PETER 4:8–11

Above all, love each other deeply, because love covers over a multitude of sins. Offer hospitality to one another without grumbling. Each one should use whatever gift he has received to serve others, faithfully administering God's grace in its various forms. If anyone speaks, he should do it as one speaking the very words of God. If anyone serves, he should do it with the strength God provides, so that in all things God may be praised through Jesus Christ. To him be the glory and the power for ever and ever.

1 JOHN 1:3–4

We proclaim to you what we have seen and heard, so that you also may have fellowship with us. And our fellowship is with the Father and with his Son, Jesus Christ. We write this to make our joy complete.

19.1 No one is complete alone. How do the Scriptures address this reality?

19.2 Which of these benefits of living in community are most important to you? Why?

๛

In summary, it is easy, in an individualistic society such as ours, to neglect this need we have for community. In our pursuit of individual rights, autonomy and self-fulfillment, we lose sight of the fact that we were created to live in community, in relationships with others.

We have seen how God leads us back into a relationship with himself. As we follow him and learn to relate to the people in our lives in the same manner in which he relates to us, we extend his ways into our world. The power of his reconciliation is multiplied through us. We also become agents of reconciliation. The result is true community—a place where people thrive because they are complemented through the interdependence they enjoy with others.

In practical terms, what does this mean? How does such a community come about? What sustains it? We will be addressing these issues in the next sections of this module. They are:

- The Family of God
- Taking Things Back
- Real Friends, Safe Places

SECTION NOTES

SECTION 3
THE FAMILY OF GOD

The society we have built is hard on relationships. The virtues needed for them to thrive are not at the top of our list. We pick up some bad habits that work against authentic and intimate relationships. Today, relationships have become disposable. If a person doesn't satisfy our needs, we often trade them in for another. Social media has powerfully impacted the way we relate to one another. It is hard to find good examples of healthy relationships.

Discretionary time has been sucked out of our daily schedules, in part due to technology. We are on the run, leaving less and less time for deep relationships with friends and family. Our lives are fragmented. We do our work in one environment, go to church in another, find our entertainment somewhere else, exercise in yet another, and spend hours trying to connect with distant "friends" over a smartphone! This leaves us running in multiple directions with no continuity between each set of relationships.

Institutions are maintained by policies and operate on systems. Programs replace relationships. Responsibilities are depersonalized. We have become so accustomed to this that we don't even notice. Our sense of community is diminished as our relationships are outsourced. For example:

- We reduce personal intimacy with God to a weekly sermon.
- We transfer the spiritual leadership of children to a youth group.
- We transfer needy people in our midst to government programs.
- We hand over meal preparation to restaurants.
- With our personal struggles, we rely on psychologists rather than friends and family.

It's not always wrong to rely on professional people and programs such as those described above, but they should not be seen as substitutes for the relational responsibilities given to us by God. Outsourcing is comfortable, neat, and efficient, but it causes us to live insular lives that are often barren of meaningful relationships. And because we are created in the image of a relational God, our longing for love and intimacy burns within us.

How much of this applies to you? How have you maintained your relationships in the midst of these influences? What should we do about this? Let's consider a lesson from history.

The First-Century Family: An Integrated Life

The primary institution of early Greek society (9th and 8th centuries BC) was the aristocratic *oikos,* which means the household. The *oikos* was a family group residing on a landed estate that included father, mother, unmarried children, sons with wives, and grandparents. It also encompassed slaves, hired workers, and craftsmen. Usually a male headed the *oikos.* He led the family, defended its traditions, and managed its business.

The household was a unit of both production and consumption. Work was carried out on behalf of the whole. Products were gathered, stored, and redistributed by the *oikos* head when and to whom he deemed appropriate. This communal aspect of the *oikos* required cooperation between men and women. *Work, family, faith, and community were integrated.*

Over the centuries the *oikos* underwent various modifications. However, in the first century, when the news of Jesus Christ began to spread through the world, it was still the basic social unit of society.

So the inevitable happened. The *oikos* (household) also became the basic structure of the early Church—and continued to be so for the first three hundred years of Christianity. In such an environment, the message that Jesus is Lord over everything was very clear. There was no split between the spiritual and the material as the church, the family, and its business all occupied the same space. In fact, the Greek term *oikos* serves as the root for *oikonomia,* which is our word "economy."

In this environment, the Christian message spread rapidly. By the time of the Emperor Constantine, Christians were probably the majority in the Roman Empire. Constantine's *Edict of Toleration* (AD 312) was a response to this fact.

The early believers did not invent any new structures for life and work. They simply used the existing social structure, the household, as their basic vehicle. The Good News tended to flow from household to household. There were no church buildings. The church in a city consisted of a network of households. The household was the environment for the church (*ekklesia*). Everything happened under the same roof. Life wasn't easy in those times, but it was highly relational and integrated.

20. From the following scriptures, what advantages did such a household offer the first century believers?

ACTS 16:14–15

One of those listening was a woman named Lydia, a dealer in purple cloth from the city of Thyatira, who was a worshiper of God. The Lord opened her heart to respond to Paul's message. When she and the members of her household were baptized, she invited us to her home. "If you consider me a believer in the Lord," she said, "come and stay at my house." And she persuaded us.

ACTS 16:31–34

They replied, "Believe in the Lord Jesus, and you will be saved—you and your household." Then they spoke the word of the Lord to him and to all the others in his house. At that hour of the night the jailer took them and washed their wounds; then immediately he and all his family were baptized. The jailer brought them into his house and set a meal before them, and the whole family was filled with joy, because they had come to believe in God.

> Western European civilization has witnessed a sort of atomizing process, in which the individual is more and more set free from his natural setting in family and neighborhood, and becomes a sort of replaceable unit in the social machine. His nearest neighbors may not even know his name. He is free to move from place to place, from job to job, from acquaintance to acquaintance, and—if he has attained a high degree of emancipation— from wife to wife. He is in every context a more and more anonymous and replaceable part, the perfect incarnation of the rationalist conception of man.
> *Lesslie Newbigin*

ACTS 18:7–8

Then Paul left the synagogue and went next door to the house of Titius Justus, a worshiper of God. Crispus, the synagogue ruler, and his entire household believed in the Lord; and many of the Corinthians who heard him believed and were baptized.

ACTS 20:20

You know that I have not hesitated to preach anything that would be helpful to you but have taught you publicly and from house to house.

ROMANS 16:3–5A

Greet Priscilla and Aquila, my fellow workers in Christ Jesus. They risked their lives for me. Not only I but all the churches of the Gentiles are grateful to them. Greet also the church that meets at their house.

1 CORINTHIANS 16:15–16

You know that the household of Stephanas were the first converts in Achaia, and they have devoted themselves to the service of the saints. I urge you, brothers, to submit to such as these and to everyone who joins in the work, and labors at it.

Our lives are fragmented into largely unconnected social groups. This is no accidental development, of course, but the predictable result of an individualistic society grounded primarily in corporate and governmental institutional security structure. . . . Along with this social fragmentation comes a temporal fragmentation. Our social architecture often requires us to work far from where we live and to shop and recreate far from either of those. Time spent simply getting from one piece of our lives to another necessitates breaking our days up into little chunks that leave little room either for spontaneity or deepening of relationships within any of our social circles.
Wes Howard-Brook

1 CORINTHIANS 16:19

The churches in the province of Asia send you greetings. Aquila and Priscilla greet you warmly in the Lord, and so does the church that meets at their house.

COLOSSIANS 4:15

Give my greetings to the brothers at Laodicea, and to Nympha and the church in her house.

GALATIANS 6:10

Therefore, as we have opportunity, let us do good to all people, especially to those who belong to the family of believers.

EPHESIANS 2:19–22

Consequently, you are no longer foreigners and aliens, but fellow citizens with God's people and members of God's household, built on the foundation of the apostles and prophets, with Christ Jesus himself as the chief cornerstone. In him the whole building is joined together and rises to become a holy temple in the Lord. And in him you too are being built together to become a dwelling in which God lives by his Spirit.

20.1 Why was the household (or "oikos") such a powerful channel for the Gospel?

21. Your family and your larger circle of relationships are looking to you for leadership. Consider what the following scriptures say about this responsibility.

1 TIMOTHY 3:1–5

Here is a trustworthy saying: If anyone sets his heart on being an overseer, he desires a noble task. Now the overseer must be above reproach, the husband of but one wife, temperate, self-controlled, respectable, hospitable, able to teach, not given to drunkenness, not violent but gentle, not quarrelsome, not a lover of money. He must manage his own family well and see that his children obey him with proper respect. (If anyone does not know how to manage his own family, how can he take care of God's church?)

> Whether your family is small or large, whether your resources are sparse or extensive, every Christian parent is called to make the home a ministry. That means educating our children in a biblical worldview and equipping them to have an impact on the world. *Charles Colson*

1 TIMOTHY 3:12–15

A deacon must be the husband of but one wife and must manage his children and his household well. Those who have served well gain an excellent standing and great assurance in their faith in Christ Jesus. Although I hope to come to you soon, I am writing you these instructions so that, if I am delayed, you will know how people ought to conduct themselves in God's household, which is the church of the living God, the pillar and foundation of the truth.

> By describing the church as God's household, Paul highlights the relational intensity that should characterize the people of God.

TITUS 1:5–9

The reason I left you in Crete was that you might straighten out what was left unfinished and appoint elders in every town, as I directed you. An elder must be blameless, the husband of but one wife, a man whose children believe and are not open to the charge of being wild and disobedient. Since an overseer is entrusted with God's work, he must be blameless—not overbearing, not quick-tempered, not given to much wine, not violent, not pursuing dishonest gain. Rather he must be hospitable, one who loves what is good, who is self-controlled, upright, holy and disciplined. He must hold firmly to the trustworthy message as it has been taught, so that he can encourage others by sound doctrine and refute those who oppose it.

21.1 How would such responsibilities transform the way you live?

21.2 Did you observe how many activities and sets of relationships were integrated into a single context? If we lived this way, how would this change the way we approach:

• our families?

- our work?

- our unbelieving friends?

21.3 Life can be arranged in a way that is fragmented or integrated. Consider each sphere of your life (i.e. work, family, church, hobbies, etc.) and the closest relationships in each area. Make a plan for creating a more integrated and relational life, and then implement it.

❧

The contrasts between our contemporary society and one in which the *oikos* was primary are evident. The *oikos* provided a fertile environment where redemptive relationships could grow once the message of Christ had taken root.

The church was not a place where people went. The church was people, called to a strong bond with one another. A first-century believer wouldn't understand what we meant if we said, "Let's go to church." He saw himself as part of the church, living in community twenty-four hours every day. The family business put the church naturally into the marketplace. The raising of children; the care of the elderly; the hospitality that was provided; the treatment shown to the artisans, the servants and the merchants—all of it was understood as the church living out the ways of the kingdom of God. The spiritual and the material were inseparable. The believers of the first century used their existing social connections to the advantage of the Gospel. What can we take from this example that can help us today?

SECTION NOTES

SECTION 4
INTEGRATED LIVING

We have just seen how our society tempts us to delegate the responsibility for some of our most important relationships to an institution. Little do we realize how much we need to keep these responsibilities and how impoverished our lives have become because we have turned them over to others. What can we do about this? In practical terms, is it possible to reclaim what's been lost? What do you think?

Much of what we're discussing in this book requires a new way of thinking. This is not another appeal to take on new activities; it's a call to approach our daily lives with different intentions and attitudes. We can recover a lot of what we've forfeited by imitating God, without adding anything new to our agendas!

Let's look at how to do this in three arenas of life where our losses have been especially heavy. We need to take back:

- Our place among God's people
- Our calling to influence people and the workplace
- Our role in society

A football game has been described as 60,000 people who desperately need exercise watching twenty-two people on the field who desperately need some rest. Too often this is also an apt description of our churches. A few do the work while the rest sit and watch. This is not what God intended for us. The church, as it is described in the New Testament, gives us a very different picture.

22. There's an insistent theme when the New Testament describes church. How would you express this truth?

ROMANS 12:3–8

For by the grace given me I say to every one of you: Do not think of yourself more highly than you ought, but rather think of yourself with sober judgment, in accordance with the measure of faith God has given you. Just as each of us has one body with many members, and these members do not all have the same function, so in Christ we who are many form one body, and each member belongs to all the others. We have different gifts, according to the grace given us. If a man's gift is prophesying, let him use it in proportion to his faith. If it is serving, let him serve; if it is teaching, let him teach; if it is encouraging, let him encourage; if it is contributing to the needs of others, let him give generously; if it is leadership, let him govern diligently; if it is showing mercy, let him do it cheerfully.

> Every Christian community must realize that not only do the weak need the strong, but also that the strong cannot exist without the weak. The elimination of the weak is the death of the fellowship. *Dietrich Bonhoeffer*

1 CORINTHIANS 12:12–20

The body is a unit, though it is made up of many parts; and though all its parts are many, they form one body. So it is with Christ. For we were all baptized by one Spirit into one body—whether Jews or Greeks, slave or free—and we were all given the one Spirit to drink. Now the body is not made up of one part but of many. If the foot should say, "Because I am not a hand, I do not belong to the body," it would not for that reason cease to be part of the body. And if the ear should say, "Because I am not an eye, I do not belong to the body," it would not for that reason cease to be part of the body. If the whole body were an eye, where would the sense of hearing be? If the whole body were an ear, where would the sense of smell be? But in fact God has arranged the parts in the body, every one of them, just as he wanted them to be. If they were all one part, where would the body be? As it is, there are many parts, but one body.

> One cannot read far in the letters of Paul...without discovering that it was concern about the internal life of the Christian groups in each city that prompted most of the correspondence. The letters also reveal that those groups enjoyed an unusual degree of intimacy, high levels of interaction among members, and a very strong sense of internal cohesion and of distinction both from outsiders and from 'the world.' *Wayne A. Meeks*

EPHESIANS 4:7–16

But to each one of us grace has been given as Christ apportioned it. This is why it says: "When he ascended on high, he led captives in his train and gave gifts to men." (What does "he ascended" mean except that he also descended to the lower, earthly regions? He who descended is the very one who ascended higher than all the heavens, in order to fill the whole universe.) It was he who gave some to be apostles, some to be prophets, some to be evangelists, and some to be pastors and teachers, to prepare God's people for works of service, so that the body of Christ may be built up until we all reach unity in the faith and in the knowledge of the Son of God and become mature, attaining to the whole measure of the fullness of Christ. Then we will no longer be infants, tossed back and forth by the waves, and blown here and there by every wind of teaching and by the cunning and craftiness of men in their deceitful scheming. Instead, speaking the truth in love, we will in all things grow up into him who is the Head, that is, Christ. From him the whole body, joined and held together by every supporting ligament, grows and builds itself up in love, as each part does its work.

1 PETER 4:10–11

Each one should use whatever gift he has received to serve others, faithfully administering God's grace in its various forms. If anyone speaks, he should do it as one speaking the very words of God. If anyone serves, he should do it with the strength God provides, so that in all things God may be praised through Jesus Christ. To him be the glory and the power for ever and ever.

22.1 What is the common thread that runs through these four scriptures?

22.2 What do we need to take back?

✍

Just as the body needs every part, so every person in the body of Christ needs to be a player. Each needs to participate according to his or her gifting. If our mental picture of church is a place where we spend a few hours each week, there is little opportunity for that to happen. Church is far more than that. It is people living life together, encouraging and helping each other to follow Christ—in full view of the unbelieving society.

Twenty centuries have passed. All over town we have fine buildings in which fine people assemble and sing fine hymns. But what have we lost in the course of our history?

23. The following scriptures were written to people for whom church was their household (oikos). Try to project yourself into their context. How do you think they understood and applied this truth—that every person is a player?

ROMANS 12:10–13

Be devoted to one another in brotherly love. Honor one another above yourselves. Never be lacking in zeal, but keep your spiritual fervor, serving the Lord. Be joyful in hope, patient in affliction, faithful in prayer. Share with God's people who are in need. Practice hospitality.

> The Church is people who are indwelt by the Holy Spirit. He is transforming their character and giving them gifts they are to use for service. Every believer is to use whatever he or she has to serve one another—and his or her neighbors.

ROMANS 12:15–16

Rejoice with those who rejoice; mourn with those who mourn. Live in harmony with one another. Do not be proud, but be willing to associate with people of low position. Do not be conceited.

ROMANS 14:13

Therefore let us stop passing judgment on one another. Instead, make up your mind not to put any stumbling block or obstacle in your brother's way.

ROMANS 15:1

We who are strong ought to bear with the failings of the weak and not to please ourselves.

ROMANS 15:7

Accept one another, then, just as Christ accepted you, in order to bring praise to God.

1 CORINTHIANS 1:10

I appeal to you, brothers, in the name of our Lord Jesus Christ, that all of you agree with one another so that there may be no divisions among you and that you may be perfectly united in mind and thought.

1 CORINTHIANS 8:10–13

For if anyone with a weak conscience sees you who have this knowledge eating in an idol's temple, won't he be emboldened to eat what has been sacrificed to idols? So this weak brother, for whom Christ died, is destroyed by your knowledge. When you sin against your brothers in this way and wound their weak conscience, you sin against Christ. Therefore, if what I eat causes my brother to fall into sin, I will never eat meat again, so that I will not cause him to fall.

> The church proclaims and embodies a new social ethic in which deeds of mercy and acts of charity are a natural and organic part of its life as it manifests the liberating possibilities of God's reign in the world.
> *Darrell L. Guder*

1 CORINTHIANS 12:21–27

The eye cannot say to the hand, "I don't need you!" And the head cannot say to the feet, "I don't need you!" On the contrary, those parts of the body that seem to be weaker are indispensable, and the parts that we think are less honorable we treat with special honor. And the parts that are unpresentable are treated with special modesty, while our presentable parts need no special treatment. But God has combined the members of the body and has given greater honor to the parts that lacked it, so that there should be no division in the body, but that its parts should have equal concern for each other. If one part suffers, every part suffers with it; if one part is honored, every part rejoices with it. Now you are the body of Christ, and each one of you is a part of it.

GALATIANS 6:1
Brothers, if someone is caught in a sin, you who are spiritual should restore him gently. But watch yourself, or you also may be tempted.

EPHESIANS 4:2–3
Be completely humble and gentle; be patient, bearing with one another in love. Make every effort to keep the unity of the Spirit through the bond of peace.

EPHESIANS 5:21
Submit to one another out of reverence for Christ.

PHILIPPIANS 2:2–4
. . . then make my joy complete by being like-minded, having the same love, being one in spirit and purpose. Do nothing out of selfish ambition or vain conceit, but in humility consider others better than yourselves. Each of you should look not only to your own interests, but also to the interests of others.

> The church was intended to be a social and economic space in which members' lives are intertwined both with each other and with the joyous gift of the Spirit's presence. . . . It was to draw people into its orbit, not with false promises or glitzy schemes but with the Good News of God's invitation to covenant life in the midst of a surrounding culture of death.
> *Wes Howard-Brook*

COLOSSIANS 3:12–17
Therefore, as God's chosen people, holy and dearly loved, clothe yourselves with compassion, kindness, humility, gentleness and patience. Bear with each other and forgive whatever grievances you may have against one another. Forgive as the Lord forgave you. And over all these virtues put on love, which binds them all together in perfect unity.
Let the peace of Christ rule in your hearts, since as members of one body you were called to peace. And be thankful. Let the word of Christ dwell in you richly as you teach and admonish one another with all wisdom, and as you sing psalms, hymns and spiritual songs with gratitude in your hearts to God. And whatever you do, whether in word or deed, do it all in the name of the Lord Jesus, giving thanks to God the Father through him.

1 THESSALONIANS 5:11

Therefore encourage one another and build each other up, just as in fact you are doing.

1 TIMOTHY 5:1–2

Do not rebuke an older man harshly, but exhort him as if he were your father. Treat younger men as brothers, older women as mothers, and younger women as sisters, with absolute purity.

HEBREWS 3:13

But encourage one another daily, as long as it is called Today, so that none of you may be hardened by sin's deceitfulness.

1 PETER 3:8

Finally, all of you, live in harmony with one another; be sympathetic, love as brothers, be compassionate and humble.

1 THESSALONIANS 2:8

We loved you so much that we were delighted to share with you not only the Gospel of God but our lives as well, because you had become so dear to us.

1 JOHN 3:16–17

This is how we know what love is: Jesus Christ laid down his life for us. And we ought to lay down our lives for our brothers. If anyone has material possessions and sees his brother in need but has no pity on him, how can the love of God be in him?

23.1 What does this teach us? Where does the life of the Church need to take place?

23.2 What have we given up? What do we need to take back?

23.3 What do you have to offer that can encourage or assist others in their pursuit of Christ?

It is also crucial for us to be influential among those outside the household. Our primary relationship is with God. As that relationship is nourished, we can enrich others, beginning with those closest to us—and then working out to our more distant acquaintances. God's purpose for us does not end with what we do within the circle of our households or even within our fellowship with other believers. God's purposes are global. When Jesus came He stated his purpose: ". . . the Son of Man has come to seek and save what was lost" (Luke 19:10). We're to be with him in that.

God is pulling together a people out of every nation on earth. He intends for them to become fellow citizens in his kingdom and members of his household (Ephesians 2:19). We rub shoulders every day with people God is seeking. We hardly even think about it. All of us are insiders. Each of us has a unique set of relationships that no one else has in exactly the same way. We have spent our lifetimes connecting with people in the marketplace, the neighborhood, the school board, and elsewhere. God intends to use us among these people.

The following scripture was written by the Apostle Paul to new believers living in the city of Corinth. In it he offers a new perspective on their ordinary, everyday set of relationships: in their homes, in society, and in their work. He points out that they are already strategically positioned to fulfill God's calling for their lives in those places.

24. To what are we called?

1 CORINTHIANS 7:12B–13, 15–24

If any brother has a wife who is not a believer and she is willing to live with him, he must not divorce her. And if a woman has a husband who is not a believer and he is willing to live with her, she must not divorce him. But if the unbeliever leaves, let him do so. A believing man or woman is not bound in such circumstances; God has called us to live in peace. How do you know, wife, whether you will save your husband? Or, how do you know, husband, whether you will save your wife? Nevertheless, each one should retain the place in life that the Lord assigned to him and to which God has called him. This is the rule I lay down in all the churches. Was a man already circumcised when he was called? He should not become uncircumcised. Was a man uncircumcised when he was called? He should not be circumcised. Circumcision is nothing and uncircumcision is nothing. Keeping God's commands is what counts. Each one should remain in the situation which he was in when God called him. Were you a slave when you were called? Don't let it trouble you—although if you can gain your freedom, do so. For he who was a slave when he was called by the Lord is the Lord's freedman; similarly, he who was a free man when he was called is Christ's slave. You were bought at a price; do not become slaves of men. Brothers, each man, as responsible to God, should remain in the situation God called him to.

> Calling is the truth that God calls us to himself so decisively that everything we are, everything we do, and everything we have is invested with a special devotion and dynamism lived out as a response to his summons and service.
> *Os Guinness*

24.1 What do you think God has in mind for us within our "inside track" of relationships?

25. How should we, as insiders, relate to the people around us who do not yet believe? Where do we start?

LUKE 5:27-32

After this, Jesus went out and saw a tax collector by the name of Levi sitting at his tax booth. "Follow me," Jesus said to him, and Levi got up, left everything and followed him. Then Levi held a great banquet for Jesus at his house, and a large crowd of tax collectors and others were eating with them. But the Pharisees and the teachers of the law who belonged to their sect complained to his disciples, "Why do you eat and drink with tax collectors and 'sinners'?"

Jesus answered them, "It is not the healthy who need a doctor, but the sick. I have not come to call the righteous, but sinners to repentance."

LUKE 6:27-36

But I tell you who hear me: Love your enemies, do good to those who hate you, bless those who curse you, pray for those who mistreat you. If someone strikes you on one cheek, turn to him the other also. If someone takes your cloak, do not stop him from taking your tunic. Give to everyone who asks you, and if anyone takes what belongs to you, do not demand it back. Do to others as you would have them do to you.

If you love those who love you, what credit is that to you? Even 'sinners' love those who love them. And if you do good to those who are good to you, what credit is that to you? Even 'sinners' do that. And if you lend to those from whom you expect repayment, what credit is that to you? Even 'sinners' lend to 'sinners,' expecting to be repaid in full. But love your enemies, do good to them, and lend to them without expecting to get anything back. Then your reward will be great, and you will be sons of the Most High, because he is kind to the ungrateful and wicked. Be merciful, just as your Father is merciful.

Our primary calling as followers of Christ is by him, to him, and for him. First and foremost we are called to someone (God), not to something. . . . Our secondary calling, considering who God is as sovereign, is that everyone, everywhere, and in everything should think, speak, live, and act entirely for him. *Os Guinness*

JOHN 1:14

The Word became flesh and made his dwelling among us. We have seen his glory, the glory of the One and Only, who came from the Father, full of grace and truth.

JOHN 17:14–18

I have given them your word and the world has hated them, for they are not of the world any more than I am of the world. My prayer is not that you take them out of the world but that you protect them from the evil one. They are not of the world, even as I am not of it. Sanctify them by the truth; your word is truth. As you sent me into the world, I have sent them into the world.

ROMANS 12:9–21

Love must be sincere. Hate what is evil; cling to what is good. Be devoted to one another in brotherly love. Honor one another above yourselves. Never be lacking in zeal, but keep your spiritual fervor, serving the Lord. Be joyful in hope, patient in affliction, faithful in prayer. Share with God's people who are in need. Practice hospitality.

Bless those who persecute you; bless and do not curse. Rejoice with those who rejoice; mourn with those who mourn. Live in harmony with one another. Do not be proud, but be willing to associate with people of low position. Do not be conceited.

Do not repay anyone evil for evil. Be careful to do what is right in the eyes of everybody. If it is possible, as far as it depends on you, live at peace with everyone. Do not take revenge, my friends, but leave room for God's wrath, for it is written: "It is mine to avenge; I will repay," says the Lord. On the contrary: "If your enemy is hungry, feed him; if he is thirsty, give him something to drink. In doing this, you will heap burning coals on his head." Do not be overcome by evil, but overcome evil with good.

Is your faith privately engaging but socially irrelevant? Is it as consistent in your place of work as in your home? Are all your memberships and allegiances relativized by your commitment to Christ? Are you acting as 'salt' and 'light'. . . ? Listen to Jesus of Nazareth: answer his call. *Os Guinness*

1 CORINTHIANS 9:19–23

Though I am free and belong to no man, I make myself a slave to everyone, to win as many as possible. To the Jews I became like a Jew, to win the Jews. To those under the law I became like one under the law (though I myself am not under the law), so as to win those under the law. To those not having the law I became like one not having the law (though I am not free from God's law but am under Christ's law), so as to win those not having the law. To the weak I became weak, to win the weak. I have become all things to all men so that by all possible means I might save some. I do all this for the sake of the gospel, that I may share in its blessings.

> People do not seek a faith: they encounter one through their ties to other people who already accept this faith. *Rodney Stark*

1 CORINTHIANS 10:27, 31–11:1

If some unbeliever invites you to a meal and you want to go, eat whatever is put before you without raising questions of conscience. So whether you eat or drink or whatever you do, do it all for the glory of God. Do not cause anyone to stumble, whether Jews, Greeks or the church of God— even as I try to please everybody in every way. For I am not seeking my own good but the good of many, so that they may be saved. Follow my example, as I follow the example of Christ.

PHILIPPIANS 2:14–16

Do everything without complaining or arguing, so that you may become blameless and pure, children of God without fault in a crooked and depraved generation, in which you shine like stars in the universe as you hold out the word of life—in order that I may boast on the day of Christ that I did not run or labor for nothing.

COLOSSIANS 4:5–6

Be wise in the way you act toward outsiders; make the most of every opportunity. Let your conversation be always full of grace, seasoned with salt, so that you may know how to answer everyone.

> By "outsiders," Paul means those who have not yet entered the community of believers: they are outside the circle of faith. This means that, when we are inside their social context, we are well placed to influence them naturally for Christ.

1 THESSALONIANS 4:11–12

Make it your ambition to lead a quiet life, to mind your own business and to work with your hands, just as we told you, so that your daily life may win the respect of outsiders and so that you will not be dependent on anybody.

TITUS 2:2–10

Teach the older men to be temperate, worthy of respect, self-controlled, and sound in faith, in love and in endurance. Likewise, teach the older women to be reverent in the way they live, not to be slanderers or addicted to much wine, but to teach what is good. Then they can train the younger women to love their husbands and children, to be self-controlled and pure, to be busy at home, to be kind, and to be subject to their husbands, so that no one will malign the word of God.

Similarly, encourage the young men to be self-controlled. In everything set them an example by doing what is good. In your teaching show integrity, seriousness and soundness of speech that cannot be condemned, so that those who oppose you may be ashamed because they have nothing bad to say about us.

Teach slaves to be subject to their masters in everything, to try to please them, not to talk back to them, and not to steal from them, but to show that they can be fully trusted, so that in every way they will make the teaching about God our Savior attractive.

Suggestions for living fruitfully among the unbelievers in our lives:
- Take little initiatives. " . . . if you greet only your brothers, what are you doing more than others . . .?" (Matt. 5:47).
- Pray for your friends. "Devote yourselves to prayer." (Col. 4:2).
- Promote the search. "'Come and see,' said Philip" (John 1:46).
- Guide them into the Scriptures. ". . . he explained to them what was said in all the Scriptures concerning himself" (Luke 24:27).

1 PETER 2:9–12

But you are a chosen people, a royal priesthood, a holy nation, a people belonging to God, that you may declare the praises of him who called you out of darkness into his wonderful light. Once you were not a people, but now you are the people of God; once you had not received mercy, but now you have received mercy.

Dear friends, I urge you, as aliens and strangers in the world, to abstain from sinful desires, which war against your soul. Live such good lives among the pagans that, though they accuse you of doing wrong, they may see your good deeds and glorify God on the day he visits us.

1 PETER 3:15–16

But in your hearts set apart Christ as Lord. Always be prepared to give an answer to everyone who asks you to give the reason for the hope that you have. But do this with gentleness and respect, keeping a clear conscience, so that those who speak maliciously against your good behavior in Christ may be ashamed of their slander.

25.1 Describe our calling as insiders in an unbelieving world?

25.2 What does this add to the importance of our occupations?

25.3 In practical terms, what do these scriptures tell us about how to be engaged as insiders? How might we begin to do this?

◆

We now shift our focus to the crucial role we are called to have in society. Historically, the church has enjoyed a position of influence in American society. It has provided the culture with moral moorings and has functioned as the conscience for both the government and the people. But times have changed.

Since the revolutionary decade of the 1960s, much of the leadership of our institutions has been transferred to a secular elite. These new leaders do not seek neutrality; in fact, they aggressively pursue a secular society. Individual rights have been elevated as the highest value, and our popular culture has responded by indulging in every imaginable behavior.

The church, realizing what is at stake, is responding in a variety of ways, good and bad. At times the struggle has gotten ugly. The phrase "culture wars" has become a familiar term. Christian advocacy groups have, at times, acted as judge and jury, rather than with grace and truth, in their attempts to turn the tide. Communication between the church and society is breaking down. Positions are being polarized.

What is the biblical response for God's people living in a culture such as ours? How should we address the moral crisis that erodes our society?

26. What is the biblical response of God's people? How do we fulfill our role in society?

LEVITICUS 18:1–5

The Lord said to Moses, "Speak to the Israelites and say to them: 'I am the Lord your God. You must not do as they do in Egypt, where you used to live, and you must not do as they do in the land of Canaan, where I am bringing you. Do not follow their practices. You must obey my laws and be careful to follow my decrees. I am the Lord your God. Keep my decrees and laws, for the man who obeys them will live by them. I am the Lord.'"

> The vision which underlies spiritual transformation into Christlikeness is, then, the vision of life now and forever in the range of God's effective will—that is, partaking of the divine nature (2 Peter 1:4; 1 John 3:1–2) . . . participating by our actions in what God is doing now in our lifetime on earth.
> *Dallas Willard*

DEUTERONOMY 4:5-8

See, I have taught you decrees and laws as the Lord my God commanded me, so that you may follow them in the land you are entering to take possession of it. Observe them carefully, for this will show your wisdom and understanding to the nations, who will hear about all these decrees and say, "Surely this great nation is a wise and understanding people." What other nation is so great as to have their gods near them the way the Lord our God is near us whenever we pray to him? And what other nation is so great as to have such righteous decrees and laws as this body of laws I am setting before you today?

> Though our sights are set ultimately on the 'City of God,' as long as we live in the 'City of Man' it is morally imperative for us to work for the peace of that city. This is not optional! It is the only way to keep evil in check.
> *Charles Colson*

JEREMIAH 22:15-16

"Does it make you a king to have more and more cedar? Did not your father have food and drink? He did what was right and just, so all went well with him. He defended the cause of the poor and needy, and so all went well. Is that not what it means to know me?" declares the Lord.

> The Jews were living in Babylon—enemy territory—as exiles when Jeremiah penned these words (below). Babylon was notoriously immoral and pagan.

JEREMIAH 29:4-13

This is what the Lord Almighty, the God of Israel, says to all those I carried into exile from Jerusalem to Babylon: "Build houses and settle down; plant gardens and eat what they produce. Marry and have sons and daughters; find wives for your sons and give your daughters in marriage, so that they too may have sons and daughters. Increase in number there; do not decrease. Also, seek the peace and prosperity of the city to which I have carried you into exile. Pray to the Lord for it, because if it prospers, you too will prosper." Yes, this is what the Lord Almighty, the God of Israel, says: "Do not let the prophets and diviners among you deceive you. Do not listen to the dreams you encourage them to have. They are prophesying lies to you in my name. I have not sent them," declares the Lord.

This is what the Lord says: "When seventy years are completed for Babylon, I will come to you and fulfill my gracious promise to bring you back to this place. For I know the plans I have for you," declares the Lord, "plans to prosper you and not to harm you, plans to give you hope and a future. Then you will call upon me and come and pray to me, and I will listen to you. You will seek me and find me when you seek me with all your heart."

> The Church could be one of the strongest resources we have for leading a balanced and effective business life. In most cases, it is not. It could provide spiritual and ethical insight about work that would revolutionize business life. In most cases, it does not. *Laura Nash & Scotty McLennan*

DANIEL 6:3–10

Now Daniel so distinguished himself among the administrators and the satraps by his exceptional qualities that the king planned to set him over the whole kingdom. At this, the administrators and the satraps tried to find grounds for charges against Daniel in his conduct of government affairs, but they were unable to do so. They could find no corruption in him, because he was trustworthy and neither corrupt nor negligent. Finally these men said, "We will never find any basis for charges against this man Daniel unless it has something to do with the law of his God."

So the administrators and the satraps went as a group to the king and said: "O King Darius, live forever! The royal administrators, prefects, satraps, advisers and governors have all agreed that the king should issue an edict and enforce the decree that anyone who prays to any god or man during the next thirty days, except to you, O king, shall be thrown into the lions' den. Now, O king, issue the decree and put it in writing so that it cannot be altered—in accordance with the laws of the Medes and Persians, which cannot be repealed." So King Darius put the decree in writing.

Now when Daniel learned that the decree had been published, he went home to his upstairs room where the windows opened toward Jerusalem. Three times a day he got down on his knees and prayed, giving thanks to his God, just as he had done before.

> . . . the only way out of violence and hate is through forgiveness and love. Only these have the power to transform enemies into friends. Only these have the power to keep us from becoming what we hate. *Darrell Guder*

MATTHEW 5:11–16

Blessed are you when people insult you, persecute you and falsely say all kinds of evil against you because of me. Rejoice and be glad, because great is your reward in heaven, for in the same way they persecuted the prophets who were before you.

You are the salt of the earth. But if the salt loses its saltiness, how can it be made salty again? It is no longer good for anything, except to be thrown out and trampled by men.

You are the light of the world. A city on a hill cannot be hidden. Neither do people light a lamp and put it under a bowl. Instead they put it on its stand, and it gives light to everyone in the house. In the same way, let your light shine before men, that they may see your good deeds and praise your Father in heaven.

JOHN 18:36

Jesus said, "My kingdom is not of this world. If it were, my servants would fight to prevent my arrest by the Jews. But now my kingdom is from another place."

ROMANS 12:2

Do not conform any longer to the pattern of this world, but be transformed by the renewing of your mind. Then you will be able to test and approve what God's will is—his good, pleasing and perfect will.

> Although our citizenship is in the 'City of God,' we know that God has placed us in our cities and neighborhoods to reflect his character and to restore his righteous dominion in the midst of a fallen world. We begin with our personal lives and habits, move out from there to our families and schools and then into our communities—and from there into our society as a whole.
> *Charles Colson*

HEBREWS 11:13–16

All these people were still living by faith when they died. They did not receive the things promised; they only saw them and welcomed them from a distance. And they admitted that they were aliens and strangers on earth. People who say such things show that they are looking for a country of their own. If they had been thinking of the country they had left, they would have had opportunity to return. Instead, they were longing for a better country—a heavenly one. Therefore God is not ashamed to be called their God, for he has prepared a city for them.

1 PETER 2:13–17

Submit yourselves for the Lord's sake to every authority instituted among men: whether to the king, as the supreme authority, or to governors, who are sent by him to punish those who do wrong and to commend those who do right. For it is God's will that by doing good you should silence the ignorant talk of foolish men. Live as free men, but do not use your freedom as a cover-up for evil; live as servants of God. Show proper respect to everyone: Love the brotherhood of believers, fear God, honor the king.

26.1 What do these scriptures tell us about the place of God's people in society?

26.2 What responsibilities do we need to take back?

26.3 How might you do that in your situation?

26.4 In what ways might you influence society through your work?

✌

We have confirmed that life is about relationships, and that just as God has taken the initiative to draw us into a relationship with him, we are to do the same with the people in our lives.

Contemporary society works against this. The marketplace operates on an agenda in which people become means, not ends. The pace of the race is such that we can hardly pause to think about it. Our purpose in this book is to help you see life through the lens of the Scriptures, so that you do not end up running the race in vain.

In these last three sections, we have talked about the things we need to take back. We need to recover our place of service among God's people. We need to take back our calling as insiders among the unbelievers in our world. We need to take back our place of influence in society.

As the Scriptures amply show, docile acceptance of the *status quo* is simply unbiblical. We will conclude this book by exploring the idea of "Real Friends, Safe Places." The purpose of this next section is to give us practical help in making these ideas work in everyday life.

SECTION NOTES

SECTION 5
REAL FRIENDS

We have been talking about major life changes. What do we need in order to move forward—to persist—in this direction? We know ourselves and we know we won't get far if left to ourselves. Isaiah has the answer for us:

"Each man will be like a shelter from the wind and a refuge from the storm, like streams of water in the desert and the shadow of a great rock in a thirsty land" (Isaiah 32:2).

We need each other.

Yet, ours is an activity-driven society. We are too busy to get down into the gutter to deal with daily human needs and brokenness. Instead we leave it to the "professionals" and the institutions. Somebody, we hope, will set up a program that will fix things. But programs are unable to provide what we need.

As we said in the last section, we need to reclaim our place in the community of believers if we are to be the salt and light that Jesus talks about. We need to change our way of thinking—our mindset. Each of us needs to be "a shelter from the wind"—a safe place.

To think of oneself in this way, as a person with whom people feel secure, does not require organizing anything new. It is simpler, yet greater than that. It requires a new way of seeing things in the way we think about ourselves and others.

We have also seen how our society looks at life through the lenses of individualism and personal success. But how does God see our lives? What does He want us to value most?

Our purpose in this final section is to give practical, achievable ideas on how to provide a safe place for others. How do we do this? And why is it so vitally important that we do?

27. Here is a prophecy concerning Jesus Christ, which he then took as his job description. What does it tell us about our condition? What is God's diagnosis?

ISAIAH 61:1–4

The Spirit of the Sovereign Lord is on me, because the Lord has anointed me to preach good news to the poor. He has sent me to bind up the brokenhearted, to proclaim freedom for the captives and release from darkness for the prisoners, to proclaim the year of the Lord's favor and the day of vengeance of our God, to comfort all who mourn, and provide for those who grieve in Zion—to bestow on them a crown of beauty instead of ashes, the oil of gladness instead of mourning, and a garment of praise instead of a spirit of despair. They will be called oaks of righteousness, a planting of the Lord for the display of his splendor. They will rebuild the ancient ruins and restore the places long devastated; they will renew the ruined cities that have been devastated for generations.

The surest source of destruction to men is to obey themselves. *John Calvin*

LUKE 4:16–21

He went to Nazareth, where he had been brought up, and on the Sabbath day he went into the synagogue, as was his custom. And he stood up to read. The scroll of the prophet Isaiah was handed to him. Unrolling it, he found the place where it is written:

"The Spirit of the Lord is on me, because he has anointed me to preach good news to the poor. He has sent me to proclaim freedom for the prisoners and recovery of sight for the blind, to release the oppressed, to proclaim the year of the Lord's favor."

Then he rolled up the scroll, gave it back to the attendant and sat down. The eyes of everyone in the synagogue were fastened on him, and he began by saying to them, "Today this scripture is fulfilled in your hearing."

The year of the Lord's favor echoes the year of jubilee when debts were forgiven and slaves were set free. See Leviticus 25:8–17

27.1 What needs did Jesus come to address?

27.2 How does this fit the condition of your own heart?

27.3 Which of these needs seems to be most acute among your circle of friends?

27.4 Read the words of Isaiah again, this time with a friend in mind. What does it say about your attitude toward your friend?

෨

Modern life is so hectic and full of distractions that we can easily lose track of our desperate condition. We just stay on the treadmill. Our sensitivity to God is dulled. But God sees into our predicament:

"You say, 'I am rich; I have acquired wealth and do not need a thing.' But you do not realize that you are wretched, pitiful, poor, blind and naked. I counsel you to buy from me gold refined in the fire, so you can become rich; and white clothes to wear, so you can cover your shameful nakedness; and salve to put on your eyes, so you can see" (Revelation 3:17–18).

What is the solution? It is to move back into the searching light of God's truth. There is no half-way house. We need to live freely in the light, in transparent relationship with one another and with God.

28. Consider the following scriptures. What does it mean to "walk in the light"?

JOHN 3:19–21

This is the verdict: Light has come into the world, but men loved darkness instead of light because their deeds were evil. Everyone who does evil hates the light, and will not come into the light for fear that his deeds will be exposed. But whoever lives by the truth comes into the light, so that it may be seen plainly that what he has done has been done through God.

> To stand there before a brother as a sinner is an ignominy that is almost unbearable. In the confession of concrete sin the old man dies a painful, shameful death before the eyes of a brother. Because this humiliation is so hard we continually scheme to evade confessing to a brother. *Dietrich Bonhoeffer* (See Romans 6:6 on this page for more about the "old man.")

ROMANS 6:6 (KJV)

Knowing this, that our old man is crucified with him, that the body of sin might be destroyed, that henceforth we should not serve sin.

JOHN 8:12

When Jesus spoke again to the people, he said, "I am the light of the world. Whoever follows me will never walk in darkness, but will have the light of life."

ROMANS 1:21–22

For although they knew God, they neither glorified him as God nor gave thanks to him, but their thinking became futile and their foolish hearts were darkened. Although they claimed to be wise, they became fools.

2 CORINTHIANS 4:4–6

The god of this age has blinded the minds of unbelievers, so that they cannot see the light of the gospel of the glory of Christ, who is the image of God. For we do not preach ourselves, but Jesus Christ as Lord, and ourselves as your servants for Jesus' sake. For God, who said, "Let light shine out of darkness," made his light shine in our hearts to give us the light of the knowledge of the glory of God in the face of Christ.

COLOSSIANS 1:13

For he has rescued us from the dominion of darkness and brought us into the kingdom of the Son he loves.

Fellowship (*koinonia*): Mutual abiding; held by a common bond; partnership.

1 JOHN 1:5–2:2

This is the message we have heard from him and declare to you: God is light; in him there is no darkness at all. If we claim to have fellowship with him yet walk in the darkness, we lie and do not live by the truth. But if we walk in the light, as he is in the light, we have fellowship with one another, and the blood of Jesus, his Son, purifies us from all sin.

If we claim to be without sin, we deceive ourselves and the truth is not in us. If we confess our sins, he is faithful and just and will forgive us our sins and purify us from all unrighteousness. If we claim we have not sinned, we make him out to be a liar and his word has no place in our lives.

My dear children, I write this to you so that you will not sin. But if anybody does sin, we have one who speaks to the Father in our defense—Jesus Christ, the Righteous One. He is the atoning sacrifice for our sins, and not only for ours but also for the sins of the whole world.

[When] confession of sin is made in the presence of a Christian brother, the last stronghold of self-justification is abandoned. *Dietrich Bonhoeffer*

28.1 What happens when we walk in darkness?

28.2 Why is "walking in the light" so freeing?

28.3 What role do transparent relationships have as we seek to become more like Christ?

∽

This idea of stepping into the light, of exposing ourselves for who we are, can be terrifying! We are tempted to keep the damage hidden, to wait until things are better before we let anyone else see what's going on. Embarrassment and shame can grip us. It's definitely easier to talk about problems in the past tense.

Our world is filled with brokenness: people who suffer from broken expectations, broken dreams, and broken relationships. In one way or another, all of us suffer from being broken. We need to recognize this—and that we are deeply in need of God's forgiving mercy and grace. He has to work in us for our good. When this happens, we can become part of the solution.

Healing—making broken people whole—is one of the primary results of God's work in our lives. The Gospel leads us into a trust-filled relationship with God. We are reconciled to him, rescued by his love for us. This sets the stage for us to be reconciled with each other. And we need each other if we are to heal.

"He who is alone with his sin is utterly alone . . . In confession the breakthrough to community takes place. Sin demands to have a man by himself. It withdraws him from community. The more isolated a person is, the more destructive will be the power of sin over him," wrote Dietrich Bonhoeffer.

Or, as Genesis 3:8-10 says: "Then the man and his wife heard the sound of the Lord God as he was walking in the garden in the cool of the day, and they hid from the Lord God among the trees of the garden. But the Lord God called to the man, "Where are you?" He answered, "I heard you in the garden, and I was afraid because I was naked; so I hid."

Again we are faced with the fact that we cannot live independent or solitary lives as followers of Christ. Individualism is out! We need love and we need accountability!

29. How do these scriptures suggest some ways of showing true love?

ZECHARIAH 7:9

This is what the Lord Almighty says: 'Administer true justice; show mercy and compassion to one another.'

1 CORINTHIANS 12:31, 13:4–8, 13

And now I will show you the most excellent way. . . . Love is patient, love is kind. It does not envy, it does not boast, it is not proud. It is not rude, it is not self-seeking, it is not easily angered, it keeps no record of wrongs. Love does not delight in evil but rejoices with the truth. It always protects, always trusts, always hopes, always perseveres. Love never fails. . . . And now these three remain: faith, hope and love. But the greatest of these is love.

GALATIANS 6:2

Carry each other's burdens, and in this way you will fulfill the law of Christ.

EPHESIANS 4:2

Be completely humble and gentle; be patient, bearing with one another in love.

> [The] conflict between family and work poses some questions. . . . How can long-term purposes be pursued in a short-term society? . . . How can a human being develop a narrative of identity and life history in a society composed of episodes and fragments? The conditions of the new economy feed instead on experience which drifts in time, from place to place, from job to job. . . . *Richard Sennett*

PHILIPPIANS 2:1–4

If you have any encouragement from being united with Christ, if any comfort from his love, if any fellowship with the Spirit, if any tenderness and compassion, then make my joy complete by being like-minded, having the same love, being one in spirit and purpose. Do nothing out of selfish ambition or vain conceit, but in humility consider others better than yourselves. Each of you should look not only to your own interests, but also to the interests of others.

COLOSSIANS 3:12–14

Therefore, as God's chosen people, holy and dearly loved, clothe yourselves with compassion, kindness, humility, gentleness and patience. Bear with each other and forgive whatever grievances you may have against one another. Forgive as the Lord forgave you. And over all these virtues put on love, which binds them all together in perfect unity.

HEBREWS 3:13

But encourage one another daily, as long as it is called Today, so that none of you may be hardened by sin's deceitfulness.

29.1 What is the place of love in creating a safe place for another?

29.2 What are some practical things you can do to show love?

29.3 Why is love so important—so central—to being a real friend and providing a safe place?

30. What about accountability? How do these scriptures highlight our responsibility for one another?

GALATIANS 6:1

Brothers, if someone is caught in a sin, you who are spiritual should restore him gently. But watch yourself, or you also may be tempted.

> The humble person will stick to both truth and love. . . . Nothing can be more cruel than the tenderness that consigns another to his sin. Nothing can be more compassionate than the severe rebuke that calls a brother back from the path of sin. It is a ministry of mercy, an ultimate offer of genuine fellowship. *Dietrich Bonhoeffer*

EPHESIANS 4:14–16

Then we will no longer be infants, tossed back and forth by the waves, and blown here and there by every wind of teaching and by the cunning and craftiness of men in their deceitful scheming. Instead, speaking the truth in love, we will in all things grow up into him who is the Head, that is, Christ. From him the whole body, joined and held together by every supporting ligament, grows and builds itself up in love, as each part does its work.

EPHESIANS 5:21

Submit to one another out of reverence for Christ.

1 THESSALONIANS 5:11–15

Therefore encourage one another and build each other up, just as in fact you are doing. Now we ask you, brothers, to respect those who work hard among you, who are over you in the Lord and who admonish you. Hold them in the highest regard in love because of their work. Live in peace with each other. And we urge you, brothers, warn those who are idle, encourage the timid, help the weak, be patient with everyone. Make sure that nobody pays back wrong for wrong, but always try to be kind to each other and to everyone else.

> One may exercise faith or hope in isolation, but not love. Love generates a community of mutual challenge and encouragement.

HEBREWS 10:24–25

And let us consider how we may spur one another on towards love and good deeds. Let us not give up meeting together, as some are in the habit of doing, but let us encourage one another—and all the more as you see the Day approaching.

HEBREWS 13:17

Obey your leaders and submit to their authority. They keep watch over you as men who must give an account. Obey them so that their work will be a joy, not a burden, for that would be of no advantage to you.

JAMES 5:16

Therefore confess your sins to each other and pray for each other so that you may be healed. The prayer of a righteous man is powerful and effective.

30.1 Why do we need each other?

30.2 Is accountability essential to spiritual growth? Explain.

30.3 In what ways can a person be a secure friend for others? What would characterize such a person?

30.4 How can you put the ideas of "real people, safe places" into practice? Where would you begin?

᷎

The following are some scenarios for how we can grow in this area of life. It is not intended to be a formula, but to spur your thinking about how we can practice the principles in this section.

1. Two friends agree to hold each other accountable in certain vulnerable areas of their lives; finances, lust, relationships. They agree to ask the hard questions about life (pornography, dishonesty at work, etc.) and to give honest answers.

2. Four couples meet monthly in one of their homes to read and discuss a chapter in the Scriptures and to listen to each other in the spirit of James 5:16: "Therefore confess your sins to each other and pray for each other so that you may be healed." Areas of special need will surface in time—and ongoing encouragement is central to the friendships.

3. A group of neighbors, some of whom do not know Christ, meet regularly to talk about life issues, using the Bible as their reference. They select a book, such as John's Gospel, to read together. The hour is divided between reading and informally talking about what is going on in each person's life. The reading needs to come first, as it creates the context for the discussion.

It will take time for such a group to become a safe place. Trust must be built. Once the group is formed, it needs to be closed to further traffic until the group has run its course—usually two to three years. An obvious objective is to help the unbelievers get a first-hand look at Christ.

Inevitably, like breathing the air around us, we internalize the philosophy and values of the culture in which we live. Consequently, we live with and are guided by a set of unchallenged assumptions that, when examined in light of God's truth, prove to be false.

The scriptures in this book make us realize that our culture has made a trade-off. It has devalued people in exchange for a self-oriented idea of success. The seeds of death are in this exchange.

In God's sight, people come first. Everything else in our world has been created for humankind. We are twice God's—made in his image and then reconciled through the Cross. Life is to be lived according to this reality.

Now it's up to us. Writing to young people, author Thomas Woods says this: "You can aspire to be one of these men—a builder of civilization, a great genius, a servant of God and men, or a heroic missionary—or you can be a self-absorbed nobody fixated in gratifying your appetites. Our society does everything in its power to ensure that you wind up on the latter path. Be your own person. Rise above the herd, declare your independence from a culture that thinks so little of you, and proclaim that you intend to live not as a beast but as a man."

That is our choice, too.

SECTION NOTES

TAKING ACTION

As we stated at the beginning of this book, the *Scriptural Roots of Commerce* is not designed to only be about the intellect. A true adventure with God, one in which we participate in God's purposes, requires us to put his counsel and designs into practice in every arena. We are called to integrate our professions with God's purposes. God wants us to live, not just learn. We need to begin taking tangible steps toward applying—at work and at home—what he is teaching us.

This is rarely accomplished alone. If you have studied this book with a group of friends, you have an opportunity to think together about how to apply the truths you've discovered so far. A suggestion is to choose one or two principles from this study that most impacted you. Then talk as a group about how you might live out those principles in the context of your work, family, and community. Hopefully, this group of friends can be an ongoing source of encouragement and growth for one another.

The following questions might help guide you in this process.

1. Review this study, including your personal notes, and identify several principles or truths that most impacted your mind and heart. What are these principles and why are they important to you?

2. Looking at your situation and context, what needs to take place in order for you to begin to live differently? What obstacles and risks do you encounter as you contemplate making changes in your work and family?

3. Thinking beyond your personal needs, what can you do to improve the lives of those around you? What needs do you see in your profession and workplace? Think about how to apply these principles in your work, within your broader sphere of influence. Be creative and innovative.

4. Participate with your friends to seek an adventure with God together. What are you learning together from your experiences? The writer of Hebrews wrote: "And let us consider how we may spur one another on toward love and good deeds, not giving up meeting together . . . ." Be committed to one another for the long-term, encouraging each other to innovate ways of doing good through your work and professions.

Bibliography of Works Cited

Applebaum, Herbert. *The Concept of Work,* (SUNY, 1992), p. 3, 4, 13–15.

Banks, Robert. *Paul's Idea of Community,* (Hendrickson, 1994).

Bonhoeffer, Dietrich. *Life Together,* (Harper & Row, 1954), p, 6, 7, 94, 95, 101, 103, 107, 110, 111, 112.

Brooks, David. Quoting George Vaillant in "The Heart Grows Smarter," *New York Times,* November 6, 2012.

Calvin, John. *Institutes of the Christian Religion,* Vol. II, (Eerdmans), p. 7.

Collins, Jim. "Level 5 Leadership" in the *Harvard Business Review,* (January 2001), p. 73.

Colson, Charles. *How Now Shall We Live?,* (Tyndale House, 1999), p. 326, 365, 371, 377.

Covey, Stephen R. T*he Seven Habits of Highly Effective People,* (Simon & Schuster, 1989), p. 235.

Dahlen, Kathy E. Quoted in *Discipleship Journal,* May/June 1998, p. 64.

De Tocqueville, Alexis. Quoted in *Habits of the Heart,* by Robert Bellah, (Harper & Row, 1985), p. 37.

Ellul, Jacques. *The Technological Bluff,* (Eerdmanns, 1990), p. 405–406.

Ellul, Jacques. *To Will and To Do,* (Pilgrim Press, 1969), p. 107–108.

Guder, Darrell L. (Editor). *Missional Church,* (Eerdmans, 1998), p. 123, 166.

Guinness, Os. *The Call,* (Word Publishing, 1998), p. 29, 31, 171.

Henderson, David. Quoted in *Discipleship Journal,* May/June 1998, p. 42.

Howard-Brook, Wes. *The Church Before Christianity,* (Orbis Books, 2001), p. 146, 147.

LaCugna, Catherine. Quoted in *God in Three Persons,* by Millard Erickson, (Baker, 1995), p. 297.

Lewis, C.S. *The Four Loves,* (Harcourt Brace, 1991), p. 169.

McMahan, Glenn and Jim Petersen. More Than Me, (NavPress, 2008), p. 63, 94.

Meeks, Wayne A. *The First Urban Christians,* (Yale University, 1983), p. 74.

Murray, Andrew. Quoted in *Discipleship Journal,* May/June 1998, p. 31.

Myers, Warren and Ruth. Quoted in *Discipleship Journal,* May/June 1998, p. 34.

Nash, Laura and Scotty McLennan. *Church on Sunday, Work on Monday,* (Jossey-Bass, 2001), p. xix, 28.

Newbigin, Lesslie. *The Household of God,* (Friendship Press, 1954), p. 3.

Petersen, Jim. *Church Without Walls,* (NavPress, 1992), p. 171.

Peterson, Eugene. *The Message,* (NavPress, 1994), p. 185.

Rifkin, Jeremy. *The End of Work,* (Putnam, 1995), p. 220–224.

Sennett, Richard. *The Corrosion of Character,* (W.W. Norton & Company, 1998),

p. 26.

Smedes, Lewis. *Forgive and Forget,* (Harper & Row, 1984), p. 170, 181.

Snyder, Howard. Quoted in *Transforming Mission,* by David Bosch, (Orbis Books, 1991), p. 378.

Stark, Rodney. *The Rise of Christianity,* (Harper Collins Publishers, 1997), p. 11, 56, 221.

Tournier, Paul. *Understanding the Human Condition,* p. 5

White, L. Michael. *Building God's House in the Roman World,* (Johns Hopkins University Press).

Whiteman, Thomas A and Thomas G. Bartlett. *The Marriage Mender,* (NavPress, 1996), p. 197, 199.

Whitman, Walt. *Complete Poetry and Collected Prose,* (Library of America, 1982), p. 297.

Wilken, Robert. *Remembering the Christian Past,* (Eerdmans, 1995), p. 93.

Willard, Dallas. *Renovation of the Heart,* (NavPress, 2002), p. 18, 24, 87, 143.

Willard, Dallas. *The Spirit of the Disciplines,* (HarperCollins, 1988), p. 186.

Woods Jr., Thomas. *How the Catholic Church Built Western Civilization,* (Regnery Publishing, 2005), p. 215.

Wright, N.T. *The Challenge of Jesus,* (InterVarsity Press, 1999), p. 185.

Wuthnow, Robert. *The Crisis in the Churches,* (Oxford, 1997), p. 87.

Made in the USA
Charleston, SC
27 May 2015